The Real Deal

'I remember the night that Rod walked into Renewal with some of the trainees from the Lighthouse. The Holy Spirit gave me a directional word for his destiny that night.

'This book is refreshingly honest; it speaks of a broken young man who found healing in Christ and a future. You will be inspired.'

Rt Revd Dr David E Carr – Senior Pastor, Renewal Christian Centre, writer and broadcaster

'Rod's story is different from many others that I've read. It demonstrates that addiction can happen to anybody. It's an inspiring read and I totally recommend it to you. You will not be disappointed!'

Barry Woodward – author of *Once an Addict*

'This book is a compelling read and one which is hard to put down. It tells an honest and gritty story of one man's struggle with the powerful grip of addiction and the absolute devastation it brought. Thankfully the story does not end there. It details the ever greater power of Jesus, who saves lives and brings about a complete transformation to those lives which are on the path to utter destruction, in such a way that nothing and no one else can. The book reveals how God's love, grace and true forgiveness turn not only Rod's life around, but also the lives of his long time accomplices and shows how that has impacted hundreds of other lives for the better. His accomplices also give us an insight into their own journey with Rod.

'Altogether, a mighty powerful read.'

John Kirkby – International Director, Christians Against Poverty

'The Real Deal is about addiction, it's about the "sin that so easily entangles" and it's about hope and the power of God to triumph in seemingly hopeless situations.

'This is a must read book for anyone suffering from addiction or who has a loved one suffering from this disease. It's a grippingly honest story of a modern day prodigal. It's remarkable that Rod's life didn't end up as just another statistic, but through his willingness to trust God, his parents' prayers and God's amazing grace, he's here to tell his story.'

Ian Aitken – Director, The Lighthouse Foundation, Widnes

'As a serving police officer, I was taught to gather and present evidence to a level of proof "beyond the shadow of a doubt". This story displays more than ample evidence of a loving forgiving God breaking into a man's life. The way Jesus' blood has washed Rod clean and given him a new life ministering to others is "the real deal". When Rod surrendered to God and obeyed the Holy Spirit, the spiritual adventure began. I knew Rod would be leading Bible studies in prison. The book documents some deeply sad times and then amazing good times. Like the prodigal son in the pig's pen, Rod "came to his senses" and went home. His Mum and Dad never gave up on Rod and prepared a celebration for Rod's homecoming, as God does with all of us. *The Real Deal* is a must read.'

Chief Inspector Gary Raymond APM, OAM (Rtd) – Christian Police Fellowship of New South Wales, Australia

The Real Deal

A life freed from the grip of addiction

Rod Williams

Authentic

24 23 22 21 20 19   12 11 10 9 8 7

Reprinted 2015, 2018, 2019

First published in 2014 by Authentic Media Limited
PO Box 6326, Bletchley, Milton Keynes, MK1 9GG
authenticmedia.co.uk

British Library Cataloguing in Publication Data
A catalogue record for this book is available from the British Library

ISBN: 978-1-78078-121-1   978-1-78078-258-4 (e-book)

Some names and details have been changed to protect the identity of the
individuals concerned. However this is the true story of my life and all other
details have been presented as accurately as memory allows at the
time of writing.

Cover design by David Smart (smartsart.co.uk)
Printed and bound by CPI Group (UK) Ltd., Croydon, CR0 4YY

Acknowledgements

Mum and Dad – thank you for not giving up on me. Your love, prayers and support over the years have meant so much and undoubtedly have played a significant part in my healing and restoration.

Emma, Carl, Paul, Linda, Charmaine, Ben and Henry – God has certainly blessed me with the most amazing family. You all hoped and prayed that a better day would come . . . and it did.

Malcolm Down and the Authentic Media team – thank you for believing in me and for giving the opportunity for this story to be told. May many lives be impacted as a result.

Mark at www.thescriptdoctor.org.uk – it has been a joy to work with you on this project. I have really valued your advice, input and friendship. I highly recommend your service to anybody who is thinking about writing a book.

Pastor Brian and Anne Hewitt – it has been a privilege to sit under your leadership over the past ten years. You have led with passion and integrity and remained faithful to the call upon your lives. I cannot express how thankful I am for the opportunities you gave me while on staff at The Foundry Church.

David and Ian – by giving me a place at The Lighthouse Foundation, you gave me a lifeline and a platform to rebuild my life. I am eternally grateful.

The Foundry family – I will never forget how loved and accepted I felt from the first moment I walked through the doors of the church. Thank you for all your prayers.

Barry Woodward – thank you so much, mate, for all the advice, time and encouragement you have given me from the start. I owe you one.

Dave Akerman and Lukas Dewhirst – you are 'the real deal' when it comes to modelling authentic relational leadership. I am blessed to have you as friends.

Jim – I so appreciate your help with the picture for the front cover. Thank you.

To all my friends who remained loyal throughout my darkest hour – you know who you are. Your visits and letters always lifted my spirit and put a smile on my face.

Thank you, Emma, Helen, Josie and Ben, for the many hours you have spent proofreading the manuscript.

To my beautiful wife, Kate – I am so blessed to be married to somebody who is completely sold out for God. I can't thank you enough for your support, encouragement and patience throughout the time I have spent on this project. I love you.

Contents

I dedicate this book to my daughter Annaliese.
I'm sorry for not being the dad you deserved during your important years growing up. Wanting to make up for those 'lost' years gave me the strength and determination to make right choices and embrace my future. I'm glad things are different now.
Thank you for your grace and understanding. Thank you for helping me keep focused (even when you didn't realize). I am proud to be able to call you my daughter.
You are so beautiful and I love you dearly,
Dad x

Foreword

Story. Testimony. Call it whatever you will, it's one of the missing jewels of the church.

Decades ago, I attended youth camps where, each evening, our hands warmed by cups of steaming cocoa, our hearts were warmed by the stories that we would tell each other, stories of how God had helped us, spoken to us, rescued us and used us in our youthful availability. The breathless sharing of our stories bolstered our fledgling faith and nudged us into realizing that all the biblical information we were gathering was far more than factual data. Our shared stories called us to greater commitment, edged us to more daring hope, and helped us to expect that because God had done something in our little lives yesterday, then today was laced with possibilities and the future might indeed be bright.

Somehow, many churches have forgotten the power of story-telling testimony and have replaced it with well-illustrated preaching and powerhouse moments of worship. Both of these are fundamentally vital, but we've lost the wonder today of celebrating and weeping over our shared journeys.

In this warm, human and enthralling book, Rod grabs us by the throat in the opening paragraphs and invites us to join him on the winding pathway he's taken.

With skilfully woven words, he strips away the myths that cling to the godless life. Here is darkness revealed in all its sombre, bleak hues. In these pages you'll find raw fear, despair, and the emptiness that comes to the heart that ignores or rejects God.

But then there's massive joy in these pages too, as Rod describes how, despite having rejected Christianity at a young age, he found Jesus, and then walked with faltering steps through the earliest moments of discipleship, including failure and foolishness.

Here you won't find a quick, flawless transformation – a sinner turned saint in the twinkling of an eye – but what unfolds is gritty, authentic hope. We're reminded that the gospel is about the grind and glory of gradual transformation.

For those of us still stuck in a rut of destructive behaviours, there is hope. For those of us fretting about people we love who have marched or ambled away from God, there is hope.

So read and be blessed, inspired and strengthened for your own faith trek as you enjoy this book.

Rod wants us to remember and celebrate this abiding fact: Jesus is the real deal.

Jeff Lucas, teaching pastor at Timberline Church, Fort Collins, Colorado, USA, and international speaker, broadcaster and best-selling author

Prologue: One Last Deal

When I heard the knock on the front door I knew immediately that I was in trouble.

I was 24 and spending a rare Friday night at home with my mum and stepdad. Mum was pleased I was actually in for a change as she worried herself sick every time I stepped out the front door. The reality was that I was withdrawing from heroin. I couldn't face going out.

It was only one week until I was due to go back to Thailand, this time with my friend Joanne. I was looking forward to getting away and catching up with my mates Jocko and Moose. They were in the process of opening up a new hotel in Ko Samui.

Only Leon had other ideas.

It was 7 p.m. and he was standing at the front door, looking agitated – almost possessed.

'Come with me now!' he insisted.

My heart started to thump.

I owed Leon money – eight grand – for weed (cannabis) I had sold for him on the island of Guernsey where I lived. Normally I was good at weighing in (paying up), but this time I had blown it all – on gambling and drug deals that had gone wrong.

But this wasn't the main reason Leon was angry.

I reluctantly agreed to go with Leon, but I didn't like it, not one bit. His eyes were red with anger and his driving through the narrow roads of the parish of St Andrews was fast and furious.

'You've betrayed me, Hot Rod,' he kept saying. 'I thought I could trust you.'

'What do you mean?'

'You've screwed me over and you're going to pay for it.'

'But I haven't done anything wrong! What's going on?' I protested.

'You'll find out soon enough.'

I tried to keep calm, but that became much harder when he stopped the car, led me into his house, and took me down to his basement, locking the door behind us.

Leon ordered me to sit down on a chair and then began to speak. He was enraged and was speaking in riddles.

A few months previously, £60,000 worth of weed had been stolen from his stash and there were only two people who could have done it. I was one of them. The other lad was another dealer. He and I had been selling weed from a haul that was apparently worth half a million pounds. At the time, Leon had interrogated both of us, threatening to disfigure us with sulphuric acid, but neither of us had owned up. Fortunately the other lad had a reputation for lying, while I had been a trustworthy mate to Leon for three years. In the end, the other guy fled the island.

Now I was in Leon's basement being questioned yet again, and to make matters worse, this time I was withdrawing from heroin.

'I know you were the one who stole the weed!' he shouted. He then demanded the outstanding debt I owed him.

Pacing up and down erratically, he pulled out a baseball bat and a knife and placed both on a table in front of me while he continued to rant. Overwhelmed with fear, I knew I had to talk myself out of this.

'Mate, I haven't done anything,' I pleaded. 'I've always been a loyal friend to you. We know who stole your stash. He's done a runner. What more proof do you need?'

But Leon was not so easily persuaded.

'Stop lying. If you don't pay me back, I'll blow up your stepdad's business and hurt your family.'

By now, Leon was brandishing the baseball bat in front of me. He swung it at my feet and hit my ankles. A bolt of pain shot through my bones.

He swung and hit me again.

'Tell me the truth!'

'I didn't do it!'

Leon picked up the knife and began to threaten me with it.

'Mate, I didn't do it!'

Thankfully, Leon put down the knife, but he didn't let up with his threats.

'I want my money and you've got one week to pay! I know your plans to run away to Thailand. I want your passport. You'll get it back once you've paid up.'

I could see that I had little choice but to agree.

'You'll be sorry if you don't pay up, and so will your family.'

'All right, all right, you've made your point. I'll get your money.'

'Make sure you do!' Leon shouted.

'I'll have it for you within the week,' I assured him. But inside I was panicking.

A few hours later I was back home in my bed. My head was spinning. I was emotionally and mentally drained. Where was I going to find eight grand in one week? I couldn't think of any scam that would secure that kind of money that quickly. And now I was really concerned about what Leon might do to my family if I didn't pay up.

The next day I spoke with Joanne and told her what had gone on. She could see I was distressed.

'I don't know what I'm going to do, Jo. Going away with you is my only chance of getting my head sorted out.'

'Promise me you won't do anything stupid,' she said.

'I promise, Jo,' I replied. But I was lying. I knew I had to act fast.

That day, I placed a bet on a horse and won £500. I thought my luck was in.

Within minutes, I had bet on another horse and lost it all. I was gutted, but the emotions of losing such a large amount of money were all too familiar.

Over the next twenty-four hours, I called in all the money other people owed me for drugs and managed to claw back a couple of grand. I could take a gamble and bet it on a horse. Or I could look to quadruple my money by doing another drugs deal. I decided on the latter.

'One last deal and then I'm free,' I thought. 'What can go wrong?'

1.

Goodbye to the Valleys

Given my criminal record, it seems ironic that I spent the first couple of years of my life in a house that was owned by South Wales Police.

I was born in Neath, South Wales, in October 1977, to Christopher and Barbara Williams. My father worked as a police officer for the South Wales Police. My mother worked as a secretary for the chief superintendent in Swansea – at least, until my older sister, Emma, was born.

When I was four years old, my parents separated and later divorced. I have no real recollection of life before they split up so I was simply too young to feel any trauma.

From then on, my sister and I lived with our mum in a modest semi-detached house in a cul-de-sac in Morriston in Swansea. My mum was well liked on our street and was called 'Babs' by everyone. She always put us children before herself. In fact, she put everyone else before herself. She genuinely cared about people, and people cared about her.

In the 1980s, Morriston had a strong community spirit. All the neighbours got on well with each other and would look after each other's children. The whole cul-de-sac came out for summer barbecues and would throw street parties in celebration of royal events. I particularly remember when

Prince Charles married Lady Diana Spencer in 1981. Every house was decorated with Union Jacks and festive bunting. People carried their kitchen tables and chairs outside and everyone partied in honour of the royal couple. The same sort of thing happened on Bonfire Night (5 November). Every year, collections were made around the cul-de-sac so that we could purchase a great selection of fireworks and sparklers. This was always an enjoyable occasion.

Being in a close community like this was very important for the three of us. We were a single-parent family so we needed friendship and support. That's not to say that Dad was absent from our lives. My sister and I had regular contact with him. Most weeks he would take us both out swimming. Sometimes we would be treated to a delicious chocolate sundae at Joe's famous ice cream parlour in St Helen's Road in Swansea.

When my dad remarried, we stayed with him and his wife, Linda, for weekends in their house in Bridgend. On one of the first of these occasions, we were having a meal at the Atlantic Hotel in Porthcawl when, during the main course, I somehow managed to wedge my arm between the spindles of my chair. It was completely stuck, and Dad thought he was going to have to call the fire brigade. I thought I was going to lose my arm! Eventually I managed to break free. But it was not the most dignified way of introducing myself to Linda, and it's a story I have never lived down.

Dad was and still is a car fanatic, especially of Ford Capris. He was particularly fond of the 280 Brooklands Capri. He used to take us on to the motorway and find stretches of road where he knew he could push the accelerator right down and not be caught speeding. My sister was less enthusiastic about this. She hated it when the whole car started shaking.

Speaking of cars, I used to love it when my dad was on duty and he made a surprise visit to our house in his police car. I would always hope that my friends and neighbours were watching as I went out for a spin with him. Later on in my life, I would be far less excited about seeing – let alone getting into – police cars.

Then there was church.

My mum took my sister and me to Libanus Evangelical Church in Market Street in Morriston. It was a typical nineteenth-century chapel which looked a bit intimidating on the outside – and sometimes on the inside, too!

Up to three times every Sunday we would go to the church services, where Pastor Rees would scare the life out of me as he bellowed forth his message from the pulpit and thumped down his fists on his oversized Bible. I almost choked on the Chewits I was eating on more than one occasion.

Libanus became an integral part of our lives in Swansea. Pastor Rees's and other families within the church would invite the three of us to Sunday lunch after the morning service. We always enjoyed the hospitality.

One Christmas I managed to move everyone at church to tears when I was asked to sing a solo at the carol service. An elderly member of the congregation bought me a huge bar of Dairy Milk the following week. I was delighted that my hidden talents had brought such welcome rewards. With my blonde hair and tortoiseshell National Health glasses, it was inevitable that I'd be given the nickname 'The Milky Bar Kid', and I soon learned to use this 'butter wouldn't melt' look to my advantage.

Whenever there was a 'bring and share' supper at our church, Emma and I would go round sniffing the food. We wouldn't touch anything we knew had been brought by the less hygienic members of the congregation. In the end, we'd always choose Mum's food. Her cooking was the best.

Church was not just about food and fellowship, though. Both Mum and Dad were Christians, so we were also taught Christian values from a young age. In fact, going to church and learning about Christianity was a regular part of life. Even though there were fun moments, I have to be honest and say that I really didn't get what church was all about and I only went because I had to. I really had no choice at that age.

The degree to which I failed to grasp much of what I was being taught at church is probably best illustrated by the time I blurted out at the Sunday lunch table, 'If I don't eat my cabbage, will I go to hell?'

In truth, I was a happy-go-lucky kind of boy who preferred playing football and skateboarding with my mates, or, when the weather was poor, playing indoors with my A-Team figures. I even had the black van with the red stripe down its side.

I enjoyed watching TV – my favourite programmes were *The A-Team* (of course), *Knight Rider* and *The Fall Guy*. Since Mum was the only wage-earner in our house, money was very tight, so we didn't have a video recorder. This was a source of some embarrassment to me.

'Where's the VCR?' my friends would ask.

'We have to keep it locked in a secret place for security reasons,' I would reply.

Explaining the absence of a car in our front drive was more of a challenge.

Since we were hard up, we learned to appreciate the good things in life. It was a real treat for us when Mum brought home a Chinese takeaway. It would be just one meal for all three of us to share – often chicken curry, a carton of rice and a portion of chips. Emma and I would eat ours while sitting on beanbags in front of the TV. That meal combination is still a favourite of mine.

Mum worked night shifts for the social services, looking after terminally ill patients. Auntie Betty and various people from the church used to come and babysit. We loved Auntie Betty. She would bring us a ten-penny mix of sticky sweets and sherbet in crisp white paper bags. She had a heart of gold – she still does. Whenever she babysat, she wouldn't leave until she had cleaned and sorted out every shelf and cupboard. Her love of cleaning with a certain brand of bleach product caused her to be known as 'Parazone Betty' in the kitchens at Penlan School where she worked.

I attended Martin Street Boys' School from 1984 to 1988. As soon as I was old enough, I was allowed to do the fifteen-minute walk to school together with my friends Andrew and Michael from the cul-de-sac. I still have night-mares about being forced to wear a graphite grey knitted balaclava whenever the temperature dropped below twelve degrees. I was also rarely out of a substantial duffle coat until at least late spring. As soon as I'd reached the end of the cul-de-sac, that balaclava came off faster than the speed of light. The waffled imprint on my cheeks would have eventually faded by the time I'd reached school.

I was of average ability in most of my lessons, but in mathematics I was top of the class. At the end of every maths lesson there would be a times-table knockout competition, in which two pupils would stand at the front of the class and answer random multiplication questions shouted out by our classmates. The first to answer stayed on. I never lost a round and was the reigning champion for the whole school year. In fact, I held the title throughout, never losing once.

It didn't take too long before my 'cheeky chappy' persona was born. As well as the 'Milky Bar Kid' looks, I also had an endearing lisp, which only added to my ability to charm people. In reality, however, I could be quite mischievous.

One time, I took an 'electric-shock coke can' to school and put it on my teacher's desk. Mr Smith walked in to start the lesson. He looked with curiosity at the can before picking it up. He then received the shock of his life, went bright red and became extremely irate. My mate Alan was in hysterics and couldn't control himself. He ended up getting the blame, but he never grassed me up.

Another time, one of my pranks went too far. On this occasion, I crossed the line.

I joined up with Jason – an older boy on my cul-de-sac – and we started to mess around, lighting fires at the back of a few garages on some wasteland. These garages overlooked the back garden of 'Wimpy', a boy in my class who was always on the receiving end of bullying. His house was also the target for 'knock and run' and throwing stones.

I was probably one of very few boys who ever invited Wimpy to play footy on the street with the rest of us. I never did like the way he or his family was treated. On this occasion, there was no other motive than to experiment with petrol, a glass bottle, newspaper and a box of matches. I certainly didn't mean Wimpy or his family any harm.

I let Jason set up the experiment, as he seemed to know what he was doing. He poured the petrol into the bottle, filled the top with newspaper, and then lit it and left it on the ground of the wasteland. We then legged it as quickly as we could and hid behind one of the garages. We heard the sound of the bottle exploding and could smell the fumes from the explosion.

The next thing we heard was a man shouting in our direction. It was Wimpy's dad. Jason and I legged it back home, hoping we had not been spotted. A couple of days later, I was shocked to see on the front page of the local paper a picture of Wimpy and his family, with the headline 'Bullies Attempt to Set Fire to Our Garden'. The article went on to say how the family had been victims of bullying for many years and that this latest attempt had gone too far.

I couldn't believe it. I was stunned. For weeks I lived in constant fear of the police coming round to arrest me. As far as Jason and I knew, the fire had been contained to the wasteland. We had certainly not intended to set fire to their garden, although I understood how they had come to that conclusion after everything else they had gone through.

Thankfully, the police never came. But it certainly gave me the scare of my life.

Not long after this, my mum was diagnosed with a brain tumour which was causing intracranial pressure. The doctors wouldn't operate as the tumour was in a dangerous place and they didn't want to risk her becoming paralysed. This meant that Mum just had to learn to cope with the symptoms.

Sometimes the pain became unbearable. At other times she would even black out, especially when the weather was hot. Emma and I always found this scary. Even though Mum was often in pain, she continued to put our needs before her own.

During the summer holidays, either she or Dad would take us to a small fishing village in the heart of Pembrokeshire called Saundersfoot. Here we would stay with my dad's mum, whom we called 'Nan Soot', 'Soot' being short for Saundersfoot. Nan Soot lived in a cottage five minutes' walk up from the beach. Her garden had a distinct smell of lavender. Giant ornamental butterflies decorated the front of the blue and yellow cottage. It was magical.

Nan was the shop manager at the local Caldey Island shop which sold homemade fudge, chocolate, jams and souvenirs. Emma and I would eat vast quantities of 'Caldey' milk chocolate wrapped in shiny gold wrappers – like something out of Willy Wonka's factory. On several occasions we even visited Caldey Island, home to Cistercian monks, taking a short boat trip from the nearby town of Tenby.

One of the highlights of these holidays would be when Dad bought the latest frisbee or aerobie and we would take it down to the beach to test. We would spend hours every day throwing it as hard as we could to each other, often terrifying the locals, who just wanted to relax and sunbathe.

Another fond memory I have is of eating the most amazing fish and chips wrapped in vinegar-soaked paper from the Argosy Chip Shop – very popular with visitors.

Just opposite, in the heart of the village, was a buzzing amusement arcade, which was always a hub of noise and activity. Nan would give me bags of two-penny pieces which she'd collected over the months and I would eagerly feed them, one after the other, into the Penny Falls machines.

Up until this time I had always disliked what I called 'brown money'. Family and friends would sometimes give me some pocket money for sweets. If I spotted anything other than shiny silver coins, I would politely say, 'I don't like brown money,' which would often leave Mum embarrassed and speechless. I soon got over my dislike of brown coins when I started winning on the machines. My face shone when the machine lit up, screeched a melody and spat out coins – yes, brown coins – into the tray below. The thrill and excitement of winning always left me eager to put more money in to relive the rush and the buzz.

Over time I moved from the two-pence machines to the ten-pence fruit machines. When my dad was around he stopped me from going on them. I now had to find ways to sneak back on – and I always did.

I remember there was a coffee shop on Woodfield Street in Morriston town centre which had a fruit machine in the corner. On my way home from school I would run as fast as I could with any change I had in my pocket. I was only eight years old, so I would have to pull up a chair to stand on as the slot for the money was at the top of the machine. I would be in there for as long as I could without my mum suspecting anything.

Sometimes I would win a couple of quid – to me it was like winning a fortune. I would then hide the money under a rock in a neighbour's garden.

This went on for about six months, until one day my best friend, Michael, decided to snitch on me to my mum. She went ballistic and grounded me for a week.

I never did go back to that coffee shop. But I would one day go back to gambling. A seed had been planted in my eight-year-old heart.

On one of my birthdays, my maternal grandmother brought friends of hers to our house. They were visiting from the Channel Island of Guernsey, just off the north coast of France. We had never met them before, but they were really friendly.

The father was called Paul and his children, Carl and Charmaine, who were closer to Emma's age. From that time on, my mum and Paul developed a friendship which, twelve months later, developed into a deeper relationship. Most nights they would speak for hours, and it pleased me to see Mum happy. Paul and his children would visit us a couple of times a year from Guernsey. Emma and I would always look forward to these visits. We enjoyed Carl and Charmaine's company.

Paul owned his own garage and had a Mitsubishi franchise. This meant that every time we saw him, he was driving the latest Mitsubishi car. He had done really well for himself and would work seventy- to eighty-hour weeks to build up and establish a very successful business on the island.

Paul was kind to us and would always take us out for meals. He also took us on our first holiday abroad, to Gran Canaria. There I remember visiting Sioux City, where they filmed *The Good, the Bad and the Ugly* – the famous Spaghetti Western starring Clint Eastwood. I'll never forget eating a plate full of ribs, chicken and steak, wearing my cowboy hat and a pistol in my holster. I thought I was 'well hard'.

Eventually, Paul and Mum decided to get engaged and planned to get married in July 1988. I was 10 and Emma was

16. This meant that we would now have to leave Swansea and move to Guernsey.

I don't mind admitting that I felt a bit apprehensive; I was going to have to leave all my friends, my familiar surroundings and, of course, my dad.

I remember the night when we said our goodbyes; it was very tough and emotional. It was the first time I had ever seen my dad sad.

Mum and Paul tied the knot at the registry office in Swansea. That short ceremony was followed by a small reception for family and close friends at a local restaurant in Mumbles, overlooking Swansea Bay. The four of us joined Mum and Paul on their honeymoon before we moved into our new house on Guernsey.

Having visiting Guernsey on several occasions, I thought it was an ideal place for Emma and me, offering far better opportunities than had been on offer in Wales. Known for its wealth and prosperity, and as a secure place to raise a family, Guernsey was considered by some to be heaven on earth. If I was ever going to be given the best chance in life, then surely this was it.

What could go wrong here on paradise island?

2.

Crossing the Channel

Am I dreaming?

The reality suddenly hit me that this wasn't going to be a short holiday but the start of a new life.

The car was motoring up a long driveway lined with lollipop trees, just as I remembered it from previous visits. Through the windows I could see the perfectly manicured lawn and the well-stocked rockery bursting with vivid colours.

In front of us stood the large house, its facade adorned with sparkling local granite. It had an archway over the front door, and the year the house had been built was painted impeccably in gold leaf. I couldn't wait to go in.

Once inside, I found myself in the main hallway which had high ceilings and seemingly numerous doors leading in just about every direction. I had my first experience of en suite accommodation. *A bathroom all to myself!* I felt as if I was staying in a posh hotel.

Downstairs there was a kitchen with all the latest equipment – two ovens and a microwave (something we'd never been able to afford before). A formal dining room led into a spacious lounge dominated by an impressive fireplace. I had never seen so many windows in one room. Each one had a great view. A heated swimming pool. Colourful rockeries.

A vast terracotta-tiled patio. Heck, this could have been a luxury Spanish villa, and it was going to be my new home. *Impressive!*

Beyond the pool, up a few steps, was a perfectly mown lawn resembling a mini football pitch, surrounded by thick hedges. Beyond these you could see fields full of golden Guernsey cows.

Never in my wildest dreams had I ever imagined that I would end up living in a house with a swimming pool, let alone on an island some called 'Millionaires' Paradise'. *What have I done to deserve this?*

Guernsey is situated around seventy miles south of the UK and thirty miles off the north coast of France. A population in excess of sixty thousand occupies its twenty-four square miles. When we arrived on Guernsey, we found it hard to find fault. Those who like driving fast might pick holes. There is a general limit of 35 mph, 25 mph in built-up areas. But we enjoyed the relaxed pace and the quaint island feel.

We quickly noticed the French influence, evidenced in the street names. We were bemused by the 'hedge veg' stalls dotted throughout the parishes on the island, selling vegetables and flowers and asking buyers to leave their money in a jam jar. Clearly, Guernsey was a place where honesty was valued and people were trusted.

And then there was the seaside! We loved the vast array of beautiful sandy beaches and the abundance of spectacular cliff walks. We particularly enjoyed the kiosks all along the seafront, where we bought homemade cakes and ice creams.

I loved the town centre of St Peter Port, too. It had picturesque marinas and a castle which stretched out beyond the harbour. The high street was cobbled, and the shop fronts sported hanging baskets overflowing with flowers.

The crime rate on the island was very low. People took great pride in making their properties beautiful and keeping them tidy. The older generation regarded it as an idyllic place to retire – with golf courses, good healthcare, and sandy beaches within easy reach. Employed people enjoyed the career opportunities and the prosperity afforded by the island – working hard, but playing hard too. Families enjoyed Guernsey because of its excellent schools and colleges. There were fine restaurants for all ages to choose from, some of them open for decades and welcoming the same loyal and appreciative diners time and again – until, that is, an instance of poor service or food caused the highly efficient Guernsey grapevine to work overtime!

What could be better? Guernsey seemed the most tranquil place on earth – and the friendliest, too.

Later, of course, I was to learn that Guernsey was the same as any other place. Yes, on the surface it looked almost picture-book perfect, with its fine scenery and its air of affluence. But under the surface there was also unemployment, abuse, domestic violence, crime and addiction. Just the simple act of opening the Guernsey telephone directory or local newspapers would have revealed this, with their lists of numbers for charities set up to cope with the ever-growing challenge of these hidden, harsher realities.

People were hurting on Guernsey. Families were broken. Some were in trouble. Others were lonely and depressed. I guess you could say that Guernsey was, in the end, quite 'normal', even if some of its inhabitants lived in mansions and owned seventy-foot yachts.

That brings me to my stepdad, Paul.

Paul was born and brought up in Guernsey, so this way of life was normal for him. He'd worked hard establishing and running his own business from when he was a young man. He started at the age of 14 as a petrol-pump attendant at a local garage. He was then taken on as an apprentice mechanic. He saved and saved until he was in his early thirties, when he bought his own garage and sold second-hand cars. Eventually, he had his own franchise.

By the time I got to know him, Paul's love of cars, and, indeed, boats, was a frequent topic of conversation in the family, much to Mum's irritation and our amusement. Paul owned a small cabin cruiser. In the summer months he would use it to take us to an island off Guernsey called Herm. On one occasion never to be forgotten, Paul decided to head back to Guernsey without first checking the tides. As the boat picked up speed, there was suddenly a loud thud and the boat came to a violent halt. I went flying to the floor. In fact, Mum thought I'd gone overboard and screamed at the top of her voice until she realized I was safe. But we weren't out of trouble yet. The hull of the boat had struck some rocks and was seriously damaged. Water was now beginning to fill the cabin. Fortunately, a nearby passenger boat saw that we were in difficulty and came to our rescue and took us all to shore. When we got there, my mum turned to Paul and said, 'I'm never going on a boat with you again!'

My sister, Emma, and I were fortunate to get on really well with our new stepbrother and -sister, Carl and Charmaine. We soon felt part of the family. Carl loved racing karts and Charmaine enjoyed playing netball. Emma and I would often go and watch them. Later on, Carl and Emma started dating and are now married with two children. And yes, it is legal! When the dating started, it did take some adjusting. Charmaine and I didn't feel the same way about each other. In fact, I used to practise my karate kicks on Charm – a habit that once ended in disaster when I took a long run up in the hallway to give her a flying kick. I slipped on dust sheets and broke my right arm. That might not sound too bad – except that I'd broken my left arm just three weeks before. I looked like a right idiot after that, walking around with both arms in slings!

At school, I made friends more easily than I thought I was going to. I really didn't know what to expect when I started my final year at primary school. I needn't have worried, though. On my first day, after being introduced to the class, I discovered that everyone was fascinated by my Welsh accent. They kept asking me to speak because they found it amusing. It was a lot more pronounced then than it is now, so that's hardly surprising. But all this helped to make me feel welcome and accepted as part of the class. Fairly soon I got to know some of my classmates and formed firm friendships with them. One of these was with Lewis, who lived just around the corner from me, so he would often pop round after school for a swim or a game of football.

When I started secondary school I saw less and less of Lewis as he started to go off the rails. I remember once going with him to a corner shop after school to buy sweets and seeing him slip a bar of chocolate into his pocket. I was horrified. It troubled me for days. One day, though, our paths would cross again, and things would then be very different.

I didn't find school life all that easy as far as lessons were concerned. I wasn't academic, although I did enjoy maths. Generally, I got on with most of my classmates, but I spent the majority of my time with Richard and Mike. We were good mates.

At that time, there wasn't the level of drug-related problems on Guernsey common in mainland schools. There were two or three in my year who smoked cannabis now and then, but that was about as far as it went. As I had had a very sheltered life, this was all alien to me at the time and didn't interest me in the slightest.

What awareness I did have really came from my dad. He would tell me stories of drug addicts and criminals he'd arrested in the Rhondda Valleys back in Wales. This was where he was based in his final years in the police force, before retiring after thirty years of service.

I was still in regular contact with Dad on the phone and often visited him and Linda, or they visited us on Guernsey. They loved the island, especially during the summer months. Things were also amicable between my mum and dad. In fact, he and Linda would quite often join us all for an evening meal at our house, which made life a whole lot easier.

Outside school, I loved playing snooker, a talent I'd developed while playing with my dad down at the police clubhouse in Bridgend. When I was old enough, I started to go down to the Cueman's Rest snooker club in St Peter Port with Richard and Mike. We spent most of our Saturdays and some of our weekday evenings in the clubhouse there. Sometimes we entered snooker competitions, but we never got very far.

The three of us would often play pranks on each other. I'll never forget the time when we typed a letter to Mike saying that he'd won £10,000 in the local lottery. We posted the letter through his letterbox at his house. That evening when we went round, he was really excited, telling us about the prize and hoping it was genuine. Richard and I couldn't keep a straight face and Mike eventually clocked what we had done. He was not amused. We knew we'd crossed the line.

At the snooker club we were taught by some of the older members how to play Three-Card Brag. They would often play for money and would begin each game by putting fifty pence or a pound in the middle of the table. As the game continued, people would either fold their cards or continue to bet, putting money in the pot in the middle and sometimes increasing their bets. When someone had a good hand, they would often throw in a ten- or a twenty-pound note – or they'd pretend they had a good hand and blag it.

I picked up the game very quickly. At first, Richard, Mike and I would just play for fun. I became quite dextrous with the cards, learning a variety of snappy-looking cuts and shuffles. It wasn't long before I started getting out my money and betting with the others.

I soon picked up the art of bluffing and cultivated an effective 'poker face' as well. People thought I was just jammy because it seemed I won more than I lost. In truth, I was an apprentice conman learning his trade. I got the same buzz from winning at cards as I used to get from winning at the fruit machines back in Wales. To me, it seemed I was reliving that same experience.

During my two years studying GCSEs I became an avid fan of WWE Wrestling and would watch all the big events on Sky TV whenever I could. I would even order video tapes from the USA that weren't available in the UK and have them converted so they could be played on a UK VCR. My contact in the USA also introduced me to other wrestling promotions – more 'realistic' bouts such as ECW (Extreme Championship Wrestling) and some from various Japanese federations. These were a lot more brutal and bloody.

I spent a lot of my spare time watching these videos. My stepdad enjoyed watching the tapes with me – although not so much the violent ones. He liked the American-style fights. To this day he still thinks the bouts are all real, not staged.

Anyway, I started to trade my video tapes with other fans in the UK. I made contact with them through a wrestling magazine and began to build a huge collection. I then saw that some people were selling copies of tapes they had imported and which were not available in the UK. I decided to give it a go myself because we had two video recorders in the house. I put an advert in the magazine and began to send out my video list to those interested. I charged £6 for a three-hour tape and £7 for a four-hour one. Taking into account cost for tapes and postage, I would stand to profit between £3 and £4 per tape.

Very soon, requests started to come in and people were ordering on average three tapes at a time. As most of the payments were by cheque I would have to make regular trips to the bank to cash them. I couldn't believe my luck. I had my own business at 15 years old and now saw myself as a bit of an entrepreneur. It wasn't long before I gained a good reputation among fellow fans and word spread that I provided a first-class service. It wasn't unusual to receive over £200 of orders per week, especially when I sent out a new video list. It even got to the point where I had to purchase another two VCRs so I would have four machines recording almost 24/7.

All this time, my mum was naive about what was going on. I convinced her that I wasn't doing anything illegal because I wasn't duplicating originals, since the tapes I had were copies to begin with. I tried to convince myself of this, too. Paul innocently thought it was a good business venture, until he received his first telephone bill. He hit the roof when he found it was over £300 because of calls I had made to America. Paying that phone bill reduced my profits considerably.

Of course, I kept all this quiet from my dad for as long as I could. I knew what he would say. My friends thought I was mad, but it beat doing a paper round as they were doing, earning just a fiver a week. As a result of all this, I did take my focus off my GCSEs and I only did the minimum amount of homework required. However, I managed to gain six GCSEs, including maths and English, so I was happy with that.

I decided against doing A Levels and opted to do an NVQ business studies course at the local college, equivalent to gaining two to three A Levels. I wanted a career in the finance industry, and this course seemed to tick all the boxes.

On getting my results, I was offered a placement on their 'advanced' level course. I was happy, and my parents were happy too. I was also only a couple of months away from driving, and Paul had already sorted me out with a Ford Fiesta – I couldn't wait to get behind the wheel.

But just as everything couldn't have been going better, I received the fright of my life.

It was early in the morning in the summer of 1995, around 7 a.m. It was the beginning of the school holidays and I was fast asleep in bed when I heard a knock on my door. It was Charmaine.

'There are two customs officers here to see you.'

'What's a customs officer?' I asked, rubbing my eyes.

Before Charmaine had a chance to answer, the two officers were in my room.

'Is your name Rodric Williams?'

'Yes – what do you want?'

'We're arresting you on suspicion of illegal trading.'

'What's that?'

'Come down to the harbour station. We need to interview you.'

Bleary-eyed and half asleep, I complied.

Pretty quickly it became clear that they thought my small business importing and selling wrestling videos was in fact a cover for something altogether more sinister. When they confronted me about this, I was adamant.

'Look,' I said, 'you can check all four hundred of the video tapes in my possession if you want to. There's nothing dodgy on them at all. They're just wrestling bouts.'

The officers didn't need my invitation. They were already busy inspecting them – all of them. It took them three months to go through every tape.

They conducted further interviews in which I had to produce my paying-in books and reveal all my transactions, as well as exactly how much had been paid into the bank and when.

'Let me explain,' I said. 'Whatever money people sent me went towards covering my costs – like the expense of buying video tapes, for example. This is what traders do.'

I wasn't sure they believed me, and waiting to hear the outcome was a nightmare. The last thing I wanted was a criminal record. I'd started my business studies course at college by now and I was just keen to get on with my life.

Then the phone call came.

'We want you to come down to the harbour station.'

I went with fear and trembling, but I needn't have been anxious.

'We're going to release you without charge. However, we are issuing you with a written caution, and you need to stop your activities in order to prevent further action being taken against you. Do you understand?'

'Yes, I do,' I replied.

'And you need to pick up all your video tapes.'

What a massive relief!

And it seems I wasn't the only one who was relieved. As I left the station later with all the videos, one of the officers came up to me.

'I never want to see another wrestling match for as long as I live!' he said with a smile.

When I got home, my family were relieved too. As far as they were concerned, this was an isolated and unfortunate event, never to be repeated. But they were wrong.

I had had my first brush with the law. But it was not to be my last.

3.

Just a Bit of Harmless Fun

They say that when you believe in God, all things are possible. Well, I can also tell you that when you stop believing in God, it feels as if anything – however harmful and destructive – is permissible.

That's my story.

Up until my first brush with the law, I was still going to church, just as I had done when we were living in Wales. When we moved to Guernsey, we attended Vazon Elim Pentecostal church almost every Sunday. The services there couldn't have been more different from those we had been used to in Morriston. Here people raised their hands in the air when they sang worship songs. They clapped and shouted 'Hallelujah!'

During the three or so years that I went there, I never really understood why people did this. To me, it all seemed like another world, and their behaviour seemed bizarre. I found it particularly odd when the preacher prayed for people and they fell to the floor. I thought it was because he had bad breath.

Seeing that I was on the periphery of things at church, it was suggested that I get involved in the youth group and go to Bible studies. I went a few times, but I never really connected. The only time I can remember experiencing anything unusual was when an itinerant evangelist called Wayne Carpenter visited. He actually stayed at our house. I was impressed by Wayne. He used magic tricks to illustrate the Christian message, and this really appealed to me. He taught me a few tricks and soon I had a new hobby. Not only was I gambling with cards, I also impressed my mates with the tricks I'd learned.

By this time I was 17 and I'd stopped going to church. But when Wayne visited I agreed to go to one of the meetings where he was preaching. That night he spoke about Jesus, and even though I can't remember the specifics, he had my attention. At the end of the talk he asked if there was anyone who wanted to invite Jesus into their life. I remember that my heart was pounding like crazy and I had to hold on to my seat to stop myself going forward to the front. I really wanted to go, but I felt too embarrassed, because I thought everyone would be watching me, including my mate Jamie, who I'd managed to persuade to come along. Jamie wasn't a Christian and he didn't attend church.

After the service, Wayne came up to us.

'I could see that God was speaking to you two tonight. What do you think?'

'Oh no, no, nothing happened, nothing at all,' we both replied, trying to be cool.

But afterwards we got talking.

'Did you feel something?' I asked.

'Yes, did you?'

'Yes, I did.'

I went home full of regret because I thought I'd never have the opportunity again. I thought that was it.

That night, I rejected God. It was now time to live life my way.

The process began when I started my business studies course at the college of further education. Jamie, whom I had known since primary school, also started doing a course in IT. Jamie was an interesting guy. He was really into his music, especially house music. He had Technics 12 x 10 mixing decks and would spend hours and hours mixing and making tunes. He was six foot tall, of slim build, and crowned with dark hair which was always gelled forward.

Jamie was so laid back he was almost horizontal. He wore Adidas three-stripe trainers, baggy jeans, retro T-shirts and a designer baseball cap. He was popular and was liked by a lot of people, including some who were on my course. Since I didn't know many of them, Jamie helped me to make friends quickly.

Most days, I would meet Jamie in the canteen for lunch and he would introduce me to different mates of his. He was a joker like me and so it wasn't long before he gave me a nickname – 'Hot Rod'! The name stuck, and before long everyone was calling me that. I didn't mind. In fact, I thought it was quite amusing, and certainly preferred it to 'The Milky Bar Kid'.

For the first few months Mum gave me lifts to and from college, but after I passed my driving test, Hot Rod had his own wheels. Paul had sorted me out with a bright red Ford Fiesta in immaculate condition from his garage. It was great having a car and being able to drive everywhere.

I was one of the first in my class to get a car. One of the others was Pony Tail Dave. No prize for guessing why that was his nickname! Pony Tail Dave was of medium build, had a goatee beard and – yes! – black greasy hair tied up at the back. He always wore brown or yellow cord trousers, a chequered shirt and red Gazelle trainers.

Pony Tail Dave owned a Renault 5. He called it 'The Silver Bullet'. You could hear him coming a mile off because of the pounding drum and bass music he blasted through his speakers.

Jamie and Dave were already mates. I sat next to Dave in most of my lessons and we got on well. Dave knew a lot of people, including an old friend of mine called Lewis (the chocolate-bar thief). I hadn't had anything to do with Lewis for years.

'How do you know Lewis?' I asked Dave one day.

'He's one of the boys,' he answered. 'We all hang out at weekends.'

'What do you get up to?'

'We chip in for a couple of crates of lager and get steaming drunk. If there isn't a party to go to, we hang out down at one of the beach kiosks.' Dave smiled. 'We just have a laugh,' he added. 'You'll have to come out with us, Hot Rod.'

'Maybe,' I said.

Dave asked me if I knew anyone else in the group – Charlie, Bobby, Brad and a few others. I only knew of a couple of them.

One afternoon, Dave drove me out to Charlie's house near the coast. It was owned by his mum and was right next door to the church I used to go to.

It was 1 p.m. and Charlie was still in bed when we arrived. That was normal for him as he didn't have a job. He had lasted the grand total of seven days on his college course and then quit.

Eventually, Charlie appeared.

'This is Hot Rod,' Dave said to Charlie.

'Why are you called that?'

'It's what the girls call me,' I said with a laugh.

Charlie was a skinhead and looked like Ewan McGregor's character Renton in the movie *Trainspotting*, although I should add that Charlie wasn't a heroin addict like Renton. Charlie's bedroom was massive, and he had turned half of it into a lounge with two settees and a TV in the corner. The floor was covered in dirty clothes, overflowing ash trays and empty beer bottles, and the room smelled musty.

'This is where we meet up at the weekends,' Dave said. 'Lewis lives here too, and Brad. They rent rooms from Charlie's mum.'

'Where is Lewis?' I asked.

'Out working on the boats,' Charlie replied.

'You got a couple of quid you could lend me, Hot Rod?' Charlie asked. 'I want to buy a pack of fags and a sausage roll from the shop.'

'Yep, no worries,' I replied, handing him some change from my pocket. I didn't expect to see it again.

'Cheers, mate. I'll sort you out next week.'

Even though I had only just met Charlie, there was something immediately likeable about him.

Every Monday at college, Pony Tail Dave would always have a story to tell about what he and the lads had got up to that weekend. A lot of the time he couldn't remember much because of all the alcohol he had consumed. And it wasn't just alcohol. He and his mates would also smoke weed and take 'pharmies', as he called them – Valium, temazepam or Mogadon. This apparently added to the buzz and assisted in getting them completely off their faces.

This lethal mix soon got them into trouble. They would go to house parties, and if one of them got into a bit of bother it meant they all got involved. Houses would get smashed up, fights would break out and people would get hurt. They became known as the 'Time Bomb Gang'. This was a nickname they'd been given by others because of the chaotic reputation they had inherited. Even the police issued a warning to people not to let them into their homes.

One Monday morning, Dave didn't show up at college. He was nowhere to be seen. There were rumours that he and the Time Bomb Gang had been arrested. That was confirmed when we saw the headline on the front page of the *Guernsey Press*. 'Time Bomb Gang Remanded,' it read. The report said that they had been arrested following a number of assaults at a local hotel. Their identities were revealed and they were publicly named and shamed. It transpired that Lewis had done most of the fighting – he was later charged for several assaults.

One of Lewis's victims had to have dental treatment costing thousands of pounds, so Lewis was eventually given a custodial sentence. The rest were fortunate not to be sent to prison for their involvement in the fracas, including Dave, who was charged with two assaults. For days this was the talk of the college, so when Dave came back, everybody was keen to hear his version of events.

It felt weird knowing the Time Bomb Gang, especially after this incident. In a strange kind of way, I enjoyed the drama.

However, this incident didn't stop them from going out together again.

'Come on, Hot Rod, come to a party with us tonight. It'll be a good crack,' Dave said one Wednesday at college.

'Where is it and what time?'

'The Pony Inn – starts at 8 p.m. We need a couple of cars, so you can drive and pick Jamie up on the way.'

'Go on then,' I said hesitantly.

As I've mentioned before, up until this point I had lived quite a sheltered life. I had been brought up in a good, God-fearing home and taught Christian values and principles from a young age. None of my family smoked, and drinking alcohol was never encouraged. Apart from a couple of cheeky pints down the snooker club with Richard and Mike, alcohol had never really appealed to me. And I had certainly never given a thought to illegal drugs or any mind-altering chemicals. That was for the down-and-outs, the losers, so I thought.

But I couldn't deny that my new mates seemed to be enjoying living this lifestyle. There was obviously a strong bond between them, and despite their bad press there was an element of respect they had from others. Part of me wanted to be accepted and respected like that too.

So that night, I decided I would go out with them.

I picked Jamie up, then went on to Charlie's, where we all met for a few beers before going to the Pony. I got acquainted with Lewis again (this was before he had been sentenced). He had changed – he was like a madman. I was driving, so I drank only a couple of small bottles.

We then headed to the party, and as soon as the gang of us walked through the door of the pub, you could see the concern on people's faces. One girl came up to Lewis and Dave and started screaming at them because she was friends with one of the victims from the hotel incident. After she calmed down, we all sat in the corner with some other party-goers who were a bit more welcoming.

We had taken our own booze in with us, and Charlie had put a crate in the boot of my car for later. It was some girl's 18th birthday, so there were lots of people. There was also food and a disco.

The longer the night went on, and the more alcohol was consumed, the louder people became. I continued to drink too, as I was a bit on edge because I didn't know many people there. Then, just before the party finished, there was an alter-cation between Lewis and one of the partygoers, which spilled outside into the car park. A fight quickly broke out. Needless to say, Lewis walked away unscathed. The same couldn't be said about the other guy.

Before the police arrived, the seven of us jumped into my car and we sped off. It was close to midnight. The extra two passengers were two girls who were at the party.

We headed back to Charlie's and arrived within minutes due to the dangerously high speed I was driving at.

'That's why they call him Hot Rod,' said Brad. Everybody laughed.

As I got to Charlie's house, I told them I was going home. They were having none of it.

'Don't be a lightweight, Hot Rod! Come in for a bit,' Lewis said. The rest of them wouldn't let up until I did.

We all piled into Charlie's bedroom to continue party-ing.

'Roll one up then!' Bobby shouted to Charlie.

'Yeah, let's get stoned!' Lewis said.

'Do one of your seven-skin specials!' another one added.

I had never even seen what weed looked like before, let alone smoked it.

Charlie made a gigantic spliff (cannabis cigarette), and after lighting it and having a couple of drags he passed it around. As it got closer to me, I grew anxious but also curious.

There was no pressure on me to have a 'toke', but at the same time I didn't want to be the odd one out.

Some of the group began to get the giggles. Others looked as if they were half asleep.

'Do you want some, Hot Rod?'

'Yeah, go on then.'

I took the spliff, inhaled a couple of times, and felt the effects instantly.

My head was spinning at 100 miles per hour. I felt sick. There was no way I was having another go.

'Are you OK, Hot Rod?' one of the girls asked.

I couldn't speak, but groaned in response.

Everybody started rolling around laughing.

'Hot Rod's on a whitey!' Bobby shouted.

It took me a good hour to begin to feel even a little normal again. By this time, everybody had crashed out except Jamie, who was ready to go home.

I decided to drive as it was late and I just wanted to get home. I dropped Jamie back at his place. I didn't say a word all the way there. I felt really paranoid.

When I got home, I went straight to bed. My head was still spinning, though not as badly.

The next day when I woke up, I felt as if I'd been dreaming. Then it all came flooding back. I remembered where I had been and what I had done. And to be honest, I thought I had actually had a good night. I had enjoyed the company and the banter, and was even up for having another go on the weed.

After all, it was only just a bit of harmless fun.

That night, through my own choice, I opened a door that took me into a world that promised everything – pleasure, popularity and power – a world that went against everything I had ever been taught by my parents. But, hey, what did they know?

I drifted away from my old friends, Richard and Mike, as I spent more time going out with the Gang. After college I would go home, eat dinner, jump in the shower and go straight down to Charlie's house.

I soon developed a taste for beer and never said no when a spliff was passed around, even trying various homemade bong devices. Now those really blew my head off.

I would regularly drive under the influence of alcohol, often with a can of lager between my legs, as we went on various missions around the island, usually up to no good.

I remember on one occasion we went to a golf course that surrounded a posh hotel. It was about 2 a.m. and we removed a dozen of the flags and put them on the roof of a nearby kiosk. There was a picture of this in the local press a few days later. We thought it was hilarious.

On another occasion, during gale-force winds – some of the worst the island had ever known – the coastal road was closed as waves and debris swept over the sea wall. Charlie was with me and we were bombing around in my car. I decided to take a risk and ignore the warning signs. This came to a dramatic end when huge breakers came crashing down onto the car, their force actually lifting the vehicle into the air and smashing us into a nearby wall. The car lost power and couldn't go anywhere. The road was flooded in two feet of water and there were stones hitting the vehicle.

Charlie and I managed to escape and ran to safety at a nearby house, drenched by the sea water as we went. The people in the house let us in and allowed me to phone my stepdad, Paul. I thought he might be able to drive out and tow my car. He did come and so did the police, but by this time the weather had deteriorated even more and the car was impossible to access. We had to leave it until the morning. The vehicle I'd had for only eighteen months was a complete mess. I don't think there was a single panel that didn't have some kind of dent or mark on it. Water had seeped inside, too.

Paul managed to tow it to the garage and, believe it or not, within a couple of weeks it was back on the roads. It was never quite the same car again, though.

Not surprisingly, Paul was not impressed. Charlie thought it was hilarious.

Things like this began to happen quite frequently, and there was always an amusing Hot Rod anecdote being told in the smoking room at college. It felt good being the topic of conversation, even if it was because of something daft I had done.

I went on to finish and pass my NVQ in business studies, and at 18 I was offered my first job in the finance industry doing accountancy. I accepted.

My family were proud. This was a great opportunity to start an excellent career in banking. The money wasn't bad either for somebody my age.

The question was . . . What was I going to do with all that money?

4.

Entering the Club Scene

Suited and booted, I was now a trainee accountant in one of Guernsey's top merchant banks. It was September 1996, I was 18 years old, and it was my first job. I was also the first of my friends to get a job, although it wasn't long before Pony Tail Dave and Charlie found work in the same industry. The economy was booming at the time and local recruitment agencies were always advertising vacancies, so it wasn't difficult finding a job if you wanted one.

Even though it was daunting entering the world of finance, I was ready for the challenge. However, it took just two weeks before I started to feel bored out of my head doing bookkeeping all day. I lasted six months before I left and joined another off-shore bank, working in a different department. I was much happier there. The team I was working with were very easy to get on with and the work was much more interesting.

By now, most of the Time Bomb Gang had gone their separate ways. Some had found jobs, others were unemployed, a couple were in prison. I kept in touch with most of them but remained in regular contact with Dave and Charlie. We would regularly meet up after work for a couple of pints down at The Yacht pub, which became our local. At the weekend we would go around all the pubs in town and usually end up in a nightclub. If one of us had scored some weed, we would end the night by going back to somebody's house for a smoke.

It was during these house parties that I would meet people who would become useful contacts. Usually they were older than me and either were in possession of drugs or knew of others who were. One of these was Danny, who was a bit of a wheeler-dealer. If there was easy money to be made, he'd be involved.

One night, there was a visiting DJ playing at the Number 10 nightclub and I decided to go. After visiting a few pubs with Charlie, Dave and a few others, we headed to the club. On the way, we bumped into Danny.

'I've got a new batch of "Sunshines", lads,' he said. 'They're the best Es we've had in a long time,' he added. 'How many do you want?'

I had heard of Es, or Ecstasy pills, but I'd never taken any. This time I didn't hesitate. I reached into my pocket and took out £30. Yes, that's right. One 'E' cost £30. Street prices for drugs were between three to five times more expensive than on the mainland because of the high risks involved in import-ing them onto the island. The courts had zero tolerance for anyone caught with drugs.

'Have a good one, Hot Rod!' Danny said as he handed me the pill. 'Make sure you drink lots of water.'

Some of the others I was with also bought some Es and we decided to take them before we went in. It was about 11 p.m. when we entered the nightclub. The DJ was pumping out old school rave music. There were loads of people there, many of them carrying bottles of water. I walked around having bought a drink at the bar, waiting for the effects of the pill to kick in.

Some of the clubbers were already off their heads. You could tell they had 'come up' on their pill by their dilated pupils and their frenzied chatting. To me it looked as if everyone was having the time of their lives. The dance floor was packed with people waving their arms in the air, and there was a lot of hugging going on.

'Has it kicked in yet, Hot Rod?' Danny called out. He was walking past me heading for the dance floor, looking a bit worse for wear.

'Not yet, mate,' I replied, but as soon as I spoke I had an overwhelmingly intense rushing sensation, along with a tingling feeling, go up and down my body. My heart rate and my temperature started to rise. Suddenly, all my anxieties were gone. I found a new confidence. I had an overwhelming urge to dance. I even believed that I was good at it (though I'm glad there were no hidden cameras to prove otherwise!). I felt I could go up to anyone and talk to them about anything. I didn't care any more. I even joined in with the hugging, discovering first-hand why Ecstasy is known as 'the love drug'.

This was to be my first taste of Ecstasy but by no means my last. The love drug became my drug of choice, and I couldn't wait for the weekends when I could take it again. At this stage I was a recreational user, just using Es at the weekends when I went clubbing. The highs were what I lived for, but there was a payback. The terrible 'comedown' afterwards was not something I was prepared for. For a good couple of days after, I would feel depressed and paranoid. I'd find it difficult to hold down a conversation with anyone and had to put on a brave face in front of my work colleagues. I'd also be convinced that people were watching me whenever I walked up the high street to work. I'd look down at the pavement so I didn't have to make eye contact with anyone. Smoking weed only added to the paranoia. In spite of all that, by Tuesday or Wednesday I'd be looking forward to doing the same all over again.

During these months my parents became more and more worried about my staying out into the early hours of the morning. My mum wouldn't go to sleep until she had heard me come in and knew I was home. There were many arguments, especially with my stepdad, who was understandably upset with my making a lot of noise when I returned in the early hours of the morning, waking up everyone in the process. I guess they hoped that this was just a teenage phase and that I'd grow out of it. They were also concerned about some of the company I was keeping. They thought most of my mates were bad influences, except for Hannah. They loved her. Everyone did.

I'd met Hannah a few times before as she was the ex-girlfriend of one of my mates. But it was when I went into hospital to have my tonsils removed that I began to get to know her better. I had to have a general anaesthetic, and when I came round I was very confused. There was a payphone next to me, so I decided to phone different people I knew, but as I didn't make any sense they hung up on me. I don't remember how I'd come by Hannah's phone number, but I had it on me so I gave her a call. I don't recall anything I said, but apparently I made no sense whatsoever and was rambling about washing machines. Hannah thought it was amusing, though, so later that evening she decided to visit me. She brought the 'girls' with her (as she called them) – Rachel and Debs.

'Why did you call me about washing machines, Hot Rod?' she asked, smiling.

'Sorry, Han,' I laughed. 'I didn't know where I was, to be honest.'

The girls stayed for ages, talking very loudly around my bed. Some of the other patients and visitors weren't impressed and started giving us funny looks.

Debs I had known from school – she was a year younger than me. Rachel I'd seen around but never chatted to properly before. I liked them a lot. They were funny. But it was Hannah I warmed to the most. I really enjoyed her company. She was easy to talk to, very caring and had a quirky sense of humour just like mine. We found the same things funny and often descended into hysterics, leaving others baffled about what was so hilarious. Hannah and I consequently hit it off straight away.

In fact, that day in the hospital was the start of a lifelong friendship. We had a lot of mutual friends. As Guernsey is so small, this was the case with many people. My mum hoped that our relationship would develop into more than just a friendship. But even though Hannah and I were very close and cared for each other a lot, our relationship was much more like one between a sister and a brother. That meant arguing like siblings, too!

Hannah lived in St Peter Port, not far from the town centre. At the weekends we would meet at her house first, then take the five-minute walk into town to meet up with the rest of our friends at The Yacht. She was always up for a night out, but she was also responsible; she knew her limits and protected her boundaries. This also meant she was a healthy influence on me.

'Be careful, Hot Rod. Don't do anything stupid,' she would say whenever I went out without her. 'Make sure you call in the morning,' she would add, always keen to know exactly what I had got up to the night before, as well as what she had missed.

My night life meant that most of the income from my wages was squandered on pubs, clubs and drugs. 'If only I had more money to play with,' I often used to think. 'If only . . .'

My wish came true a short time later.

One Friday evening, Danny asked me to meet him at a car park. 'I want to talk to you about something,' he said.

Thinking that he was merely wanting to sell me more Ecstasy pills, I agreed.

When I arrived, he passed me a small bag.

'There's thirty Jack and Jills in there,' he said. 'You can have them at twenty fives if you want.'

I did the maths in my head. Thirty pills ('Jack and Jills') at £25 each was £750.

'I haven't got that kind of money,' I replied.

'You can pay me after the weekend, if you like,' Danny said. 'You can give me the money on Monday.'

Again my pocket calculator of a brain kicked into action. *If I sell twenty-five pills at £30, then either I can keep five pills and take them myself, or I can sell the five and make £150 – a tidy little profit. Or I can do a bit of both. Either way, the pills won't be hard to sell. I know they're a good batch because I've taken them myself.*

I looked at Dan.

'Thanks, mate,' I said. 'I'll give you the cash on Monday.'

As I walked away with the bag, all I could think was *Easy money!*

I made a few phone calls to potential customers, and that night all the pills went within a couple of hours, apart from two which I kept for myself. I went home and hid the money in a video case in my bedroom, ready to weigh in on Monday. Danny was going to be happy.

And he was.

'Same again this weekend, Hot Rod,' Danny said, as he took delivery of the £750 on Monday.

'For sure,' I replied.

'Come and see me Friday night and I'll sort you out,' Danny quipped. So that weekend I picked up and sold more.

And so it went on in the weeks that followed.

It was never a problem selling pills as my network of customers was growing. My only big challenge was trying not to consume all the profits myself. I would try to wait until there were no pills left, except my personal ones, before taking any. But in practice this rarely happened. In fact, it was more usual than not for me to be completely wasted by 9 p.m. Taking at least three or four pills during the night became normal, along with whatever other drugs were being passed around. I was in such a bad state in the early hours of one morning that Rachel found me sitting on the steps of a shop talking to a rubbish bin. Apparently, the pills I had taken that night were mixed with ketamine (a horse tranquilizer). I was on another planet.

To be honest, during this time I never considered myself a criminal. *If they're not going to get them off me, they'll get them off someone else.* That's what I used to think, trying to justify my actions. But the truth was, I was breaking the law. I was a criminal. It was just that I didn't see myself that way. And I never thought I'd go to prison. The police weren't going to suspect an innocent-looking bank worker like me.

Why did I do it?

I have often been asked that question over the years. I didn't really *need* the money, and yet, at the same time, I wasn't satisfied with what I had. I was greedy. And when I saw the bundles of cash piled up after a weekend's business, it sparked an unhealthy craving for more. I was pursuing wealth, and my pursuit was increasing in momentum.

If money was one reason, the buzz was another. I enjoyed the rush of going into a club or a pub and seeing people flock to me because they knew that I had something that could supposedly make their night better. That gave me a sense of self-importance and power. I felt popular, plus I was making a lot of money. I'd always be invited to the different parties that went on after the clubs had shut. Sometimes, the famous DJs who'd been playing at the clubs would be there. It was as if I was a person of significance, that I had arrived, that I had earned the respect of loads of people. How deceived I was. Far from being on the road to riches, I was on a slippery slope towards disaster. It was only a matter of time.

My lust for 'more' grew, until one day I opened a door to another addiction – the bookies. Meeting a couple of mates in a lunch break, I ended up betting on a horse, and that was it. I was hooked. I had dabbled with cards and fruit machines, but this was a whole different ball game. There was potentially more to win gambling this way – or more to lose, depending on how you look at it. Every spare minute I had, I would be in the bookies placing bets on horses, dogs, football, motor racing – basically, anything that moved. I even created a few of my own betting formulas, believing I could beat the system. I never did.

I knew I had a problem. When I had a cigarette break at work I'd dash to the nearest bookies to place a quick bet. On Saturdays I would spend up to seven hours in the betting shop, determined not to miss a single bet. Some days I won several hundred pounds. Other days I would lose double that. That's how bad it became. Placing a bet of £500 on a horse became a common practice. I never noticed that my good days, the days on which I won, were greatly outnumbered by my bad days. Mostly I would lose, and lose big. I could receive my monthly salary one day and lose the whole lot at the bookies the next. Time after time I would experience the gut-wrenching feeling of losing all my cash.

Given that addictions lead into progressively greater darkness, it's probably no surprise that things deteriorated.

In late 1999, my stepdad thought it would be a good idea for me to climb on to the property ladder, and he helped me do that by putting down a large deposit on a house. While I really appreciated his wisdom and generosity, I was also very anxious because I knew this meant I was going to have to learn to be responsible with money – to pay the mortgage, the bills, for food, and so on. I was not exactly self-disciplined or prudent with money, so this was a very real fear.

The house in question was a new build on a new development in the parish of St Saviour's. The house overlooked the runway of Guernsey Airport. This fabulous little two-bedroom property was clean with bright magnolia walls and new white goods – fridge, freezer, washer and so on. The carpets were the light beige colour that demanded you take your shoes off before entering. Yes, I was very fortunate to have such a nice house. The question was, how long would it stay this way?

Hannah was really thrilled and saw it as a great opportunity for me. I didn't let on to her the full extent of my drug use and gambling. It wouldn't be long, however, before she would find out the truth.

Not long after moving into my house, my extra-curricular lifestyle choices began to take their toll. I was out at a nightclub one evening when I was jumped on by two bouncers for looking 'suspicious'. They took me into their office and searched me. They found two Ecstasy pills, 23 grams of weed and about £600 in cash. I was arrested and later charged on two accounts for possession of a controlled substance. While being dragged through the club by the bouncers, I'd swallowed 3 or 4 grams of the weed. About an hour later, I passed out in a holding cell at the police station. I came round minutes later, lying on the floor in the recovery position outside the station and surrounded by paramedics. I was taken to the hospital for examination until the on-duty doctor was satisfied that I was OK. I was later told that there was another person in the cell with me who had pressed the emergency buzzer when he saw my body hit the ground. He may have saved my life. The police tried to charge me with 'intent to supply', but the bookies came to my rescue, confirming that I had won the best part of that sum that day on the horses. That was actually true.

The following day, my house was searched by police and customs officers. I was so ashamed. What were my neighbours going to think? When my family found out, they were devastated. No matter how hard I tried, playing the 'innocent' card just didn't work. They were angry, disappointed and concerned. My mum told me she couldn't take any more worry and pleaded with me to stop what I was doing. She would keep telling me she was praying for me. This made me feel so uncomfortable and always made me storm off before I reacted and said something I would regret. My dad, being an ex-police inspector, had had his suspicions already, but this was just the confirmation he needed to fly over to the island to challenge me face to face. He was doing what any concerned dad would have done, although I didn't welcome his visit. He even played the 'God' card too.

My boss at work took it all surprisingly well and was very gracious, giving me a second chance and offering as much support as was needed. He even wrote a glowing character reference for my court hearing. My previous boss kindly did the same.

I escaped a prison sentence but received a £1,300 fine. Worse still, I now had a criminal record, with two drugs offences. I couldn't pretend I wasn't a criminal – not any more.

5.

Slippery Slope

It's true when they say that 'actions speak louder than words'. My actions after my drugs conviction spoke volumes. Within days I was back in the game.

It was during a night out that I was introduced to a guy called Leon. He had recently returned to the island after serving a prison sentence in the UK. Leon was around six foot one, of slim build, with thick dark hair and was always clean shaven. With an expensive taste in clothes he was always well dressed, as he was overly conscious of his appearance. One feature he could never hide, though, were the prominent dark bags he had under his eyes. He was disliked by many who'd known him before he went down. I had never seen or heard of him, so I started chatting to him. It was obvious that he had some problems. He had some strong views, too. He hated the authorities and blamed them entirely for the years he'd lost in prison. He was very bitter and wanted revenge, and he wasn't going to stop until he got it.

Leon used a lot of diazepam (Valium). Without it, he would have been very unstable. He had heard of my involvement with Danny and described him as small fish compared with what he was capable of doing. That caught my attention. I saw the pound sign flash in front of me.

Soon after meeting Leon, I changed jobs and now started working for a different bank outside the main town. I was also on a better salary. I now began to spend more of my spare time with him.

Leon respected and was fascinated by some of the villains and gangsters from the London underworld. He would read books on the Kray twins and those associated with them. Stories of crime, drug deals and violence seemed to inspire him. He would talk the talk himself, but I wasn't sure if it was just words as I didn't really know him. However, all the talk clearly rubbed off on me. I now began to read these books too.

As we got to know each other better, Leon began to warn me to stay away from Danny, as he didn't trust him. 'I can sort you out with anything you want at a cheaper price. Just be patient,' he said.

I wasn't good at being patient, so in the meantime I grabbed everything I could get my hands on – Ecstasy, speed, weed, cocaine, anything I could make money from.

Cocaine was always difficult to get hold of and very rarely available in Guernsey. It was also very expensive. I'm sure if there had been a regular supply, it would have replaced Ecstasy as my drug of choice.

The first time I tried cocaine was when I was given some by Mickey at a house of a mutual friend. Mickey was a Brummie (from Birmingham) and would visit the island regularly. He was black, approximately six foot and of medium build. He liked his gold and always wore expensive designer clothes. Mickey was a good contact to have, and I would also prove to be useful to him in the future in more ways than one.

By now, my network of contacts had begun to grow. I started to meet people well known in the criminal underworld on the island. I became more aware of the risks of being seen with people who were likely to be on the police's 'hit list'. Since my arrest and conviction I had become paranoid about being watched by the police. I was convinced my house was under surveillance and that my phones were being tapped. They probably were.

Leon eventually came through with his promises and said he had a 'big' delivery of pills that would last for months.

'I'll let you have them a lot more cheaply than the price Danny's given them to you at.'

'Sorted,' I replied.

Week after week, the pubs and clubs were now flooded with new 'Mitsubishi'-stamped pills and the cash began to pile up. Tens of thousands of pounds came in. Leon was making a mint. There were several people selling for him, but Leon trusted me the most. At first, I was good at paying Leon what he was due – but as my gambling became more and more out of control, I started to gamble the money that was meant for Leon. I would then have to think of ways to make the money back when I lost. I did this a number of ways – by taking out loans, using credit cards and scamming my family out of money. I always seemed to manage to scrape through at the last minute. Paying up was my top priority. I didn't want to find myself on the wrong side of Leon. I had spent enough time with him to know what he was capable of.

All the while, I convinced myself that one day soon I would strike gold and have more money than I would know what to do with. *The big win on the horses isn't far off,* I would tell myself. In that respect, I was no different from every other gambling addict – living under the false illusion of a future windfall.

My mate Lennie was just like that. In fact, in him I met my match when it came to gambling. I first met Lennie one night when I was in a club selling Ecstasy pills that just happened to be fake – another scam of mine to make money. I would always be careful about choosing who I'd rip off, but Lennie and his mates looked like easy targets when I saw them in the club. And they were.

'Are you looking for anything for tonight?' I said to Lennie.

'What you got?'

'New pills, just hit the island, mate, and they're going fast,' I replied. 'I know somebody in here with a few left. I can go and see if he still has some,' I added, just to cover my tracks.

'I'll have three, and they'd better be good,' Lennie said. He handed me £75.

After walking around the club for five minutes, pretending I was taking delivery of the pills from someone else, I gave Lennie and his mates the pills.

'Enjoy, lads!' I said. I then left the club, just in case there was any comeback.

The next day, I was in the bookies, and who should walk in but Lennie.

'You ripped us off last night! I want my money back!'

'As far as I knew, they were the real thing. Nothing to do with me – I was just the middle man,' I said.

'I know that old trick. I do it myself,' he said, smiling. 'I tell you what, if you just give me fifty quid, I won't say anything.'

'Deal,' I said, as I handed him the money.

Within minutes, he had lost it on a greyhound.

A friendship was formed that day. Lennie and I had a lot in common. He liked gambling, taking drugs and partying, and was always interested in making money. Losing hundreds of pounds a day in the bookies was the norm for him too.

Meanwhile, Leon began telling me I was mad for throwing my money away on gambling. He would even show some concern about my excessive use of Ecstasy. I don't know whether that was genuine or just anxiety about me getting arrested and him losing out.

Whatever the reason, Leon was right to be concerned. Towards the end of 2000, I went on a six-month binge of drinking alcohol and taking Ecstasy almost every night. This was with a girl I used to work with in my previous job. Mel was always up for a mad one. She had long blonde hair and was petite in size. At the time, I was impressed by how much alcohol she could drink because of how small she was. Straight after work we would go to a pub and stay out all evening drinking, before heading off to a nightclub until the early hours, sometimes only having a couple of hours' sleep before having to get up for work. That wasn't good for my mental state or hers.

Mel lived in the centre of town, which was ideal. It meant I had a safe house for my gear (drugs) and wouldn't have far to go if I needed to top up. Mel was not always aware of my stash in her flat as I didn't want her to get into trouble. The less she knew, the better.

In the early hours of one Saturday morning, we were leaving town and going back to my house. I was driving. A friend known as Bonehead was also in the vehicle. As we were going through the back lanes by the hospital I noticed a car following behind. The next minute, blue lights started flashing. There was no way I was pulling over. I had my reasons. I had to get away. And so began a high-speed police chase.

I drove at double the speed limit along Bailiff's Cross Road, with the police in hot pursuit. I decided to try to lose them down the winding, narrow lanes which I knew like the back of my hand. It worked. I got away.

I quickly ditched my car at a hotel near my house and left the keys in it to make it look as if it had been stolen by joyriders.

Strangely enough, I never did get pulled in for it.

Bonehead and Mel vowed never to get in the car with me again. Good job, as not long after this I was driving home by myself from a night out and I lost control of the car, which ended up bouncing off two walls, while I careered head-first into and almost through the windscreen, shattering it in the process. I wasn't wearing a seatbelt. There was blood everywhere. This resulted in another visit to the hospital and another lucky escape from the law.

My head looked like a road map for weeks after. The car was a write-off and I was fortunate to be alive. Was somebody looking out for me?

During this chaotic period, I developed sleep paralysis. Whenever I went to bed and fell asleep, I would wake not long afterwards, unable to move and gripped by an overwhelming fear, not even being able to speak or scream. It was as though somebody was pinning me to the bed, or a heavy weight was sitting on my chest with somebody trying to choke me. I was convinced there was an 'evil' force in the room terrorizing me.

I had never experienced anything like it, nor have I since. I put it down to the number of Es I was taking, so cut down drastically. After four or five months of sleeping hell, it stopped.

The more chaotic my life became, the less time I spent around my family. I purposely distanced myself from them. I couldn't bear the thought of them discovering the full extent of my crazy existence. I knew it would tear them apart even more. During quieter moments I really did miss them, but I couldn't cope with the punishing guilt I experienced when I was in their presence. Avoidance was my way of coping. It was easier for me to stay away and block out my emotions, refusing to feel the hurt and pain I was causing them.

But this couldn't go on for ever.

One day, I received a phone call from my sister, Emma.

'Rod, Mum is in hospital. We think she's had a stroke.'

My heart sank. 'Is she OK?'

'I don't know. If you want to see her, I'll pick you up in half an hour.'

'Of course I want to see her!'

'Make sure you're ready. I'm not waiting around for you.'

My heart was racing. I could only think the worst. Was she going to be OK? Had this happened because of all the worry I'd caused her?

My mind was in turmoil. I couldn't stay away from my parents now.

When I arrived at the hospital, I rushed to Mum's ward and to her bedside. She looked so fragile and vulnerable, almost child-like. She seemed confused, and her speech sounded different.

As soon as she saw me, she held out her hand. I grasped it tightly and gave her a smile.

'Hi, Mum, you're in the best place. You'll be OK. Don't worry.'

Outwardly, I sounded positive – but inside I felt crushed. Seeing my mum like this, I could feel the emotions that I'd suppressed begin to well up in my heart. I tried my hardest to fight them and stay in control.

When I got home later the relief was immense. I couldn't fight the tears back any longer and I broke down. I remember very vividly saying a prayer for her. I was desperate. There was nowhere else to turn.

Mum was flown by air ambulance to Southampton General Hospital the next morning for further examinations by the neurosurgeons. Our fears were confirmed: her brain tumour had haemorrhaged.

After an initial biopsy, Mum was booked into theatre to have her tumour removed. There was a very real possibility that she would be in a wheelchair for the rest of her life. There was also a high risk that her eyesight would not be restored to what it had been before the haemorrhage.

I travelled with the rest of my family to Southampton and spent a couple of days with my mum at the hospital before her operation. The operation, although long, went smoothly. The surgeon removed the tumour, which was the size of a golf ball. However, he confirmed that her eyesight had been irreparably damaged.

After just a couple of weeks on the neuro ward, Mum was able to return to Guernsey to recuperate. Following several weeks of nursing in two local hospitals, she was finally allowed home.

The invasive surgery had taken its toll on her body; my mum has never had a full and total recovery to this day.

Everyday simple tasks were now a major challenge. But at least she was still alive.

Maybe there was a God after all.

6.

Chasing the Dragon

It's often said that 'money is the root of all evil'. That's wrong. We need money to buy the bare necessities of life. Money in itself is therefore morally neutral. It is the *love of money* which is the root of all evil, not money itself. When people start pursuing the accumulation of wealth for personal greed, that is a lifestyle choice which inevitably leads them into darkness.

This is a perfect description of my life at this time. I had descended into a dark pit of what the Bible calls idolatry and we call 'addiction'. I was obsessed with gambling and increasingly involved in criminal behaviour. I foolishly believed the lie that this was the answer to life.

If I thought that I was pulling the wool over everyone's eyes, I had another think coming. My dad was already aware that my gambling was now a serious problem. He went all out to put a stop to it.

On one of his visits to Guernsey, he went to all the betting shops on the island and told the managers they were to stop serving me. 'You're helping to ruin my son's life,' he said to them. He even designed a 'warning' poster with my photo on it. It said that gambling was wrecking my life. I had no idea he'd done this until one day when I went into one of the bookies in the town centre. The manager came out to see me.

'We can't let you place a bet here,' he said. 'Your dad's visited us and has asked us not to serve you.'

I was absolutely raging. I couldn't believe it.

I went to every betting shop I knew. I met with the same response everywhere.

Why can't Dad just stay out of my business! I thought.

For weeks I was filled with hatred towards him. I wouldn't speak to him. I refused to answer the phone when he called. I was livid.

The psychologists say that anger is the negative emotion you feel when one of your goals has been blocked. Well, that was what I was experiencing. I was furious that Dad had blocked me from placing bets and from trying to accumulate more money.

However, the mind of an addict is extraordinarily inventive in overcoming every obstacle. In my case, my frustration was alleviated one day when my line manager introduced me to online betting. He had no idea how serious my addiction was, and so for him it was just a casual remark. For me, however, it was a lifeline. I had found a way of gambling which didn't involve visiting betting shops. I had thwarted my dad's attempts to obstruct me. My rage began to subside.

From that day on, I had a reason to look forward to going to work. My computer there had Internet access. That meant that I could place bets throughout the day. The problem was that I was using my credit and debit cards. When you're handing cash over a counter, you're more aware of what you're spending. With cards online, you bet big with a greater recklessness. As a result, I sometimes lost up to £1,000 in an afternoon.

How much did I lose during this phase of unrestrained gambling? I don't know for sure, but looking back I wouldn't be at all surprised if it was close to £150,000. That's how bad it was.

On one occasion, I took a psychiatric evaluation when I was trying to find help for my compulsive behaviour. I was diagnosed as a 'pathological gambler'. When I heard that description I refused to accept it. My betting was just a hobby. I was in control. I was simply waiting for the one big win that was just round the corner. When that came through, I would stop for ever. No problem.

Of course, it didn't help that Leon was fulfilling his dream of getting 'filthy rich'. I was jealous of him. If he could do it, why couldn't I?

Having said that, I did notice one thing about him. Even though he had loads of money, he was still a very angry person. His money didn't seem to make him happy.

By now, Leon and I were close mates. I was the person he trusted more than anyone. At the time, there was another lad in our world who wasn't trustworthy – not one little bit. His name was Tony. He wanted to be 'Mr Big' and he worked for Leon. I didn't trust him any further than I could have thrown him. He was a compulsive liar and had a big mouth. I warned Leon not to trust him and to make sure that he wasn't in the loop if he was planning anything big. But Leon didn't listen.

I had an idea that Leon was thinking of attempting something beyond what had become ordinary. It was obvious from the way he was acting and talking. Although I warned against it, Leon wanted to involve Tony as well.

I had no idea how big Leon was thinking until one morning, he asked me to meet him at his flat. He looked as if he'd been up all night. He had.

'I told you I would do it one day, Hot Rod!' Leon said.

'Do what?' I asked, with a quizzical look on my face.

'Half a million, that's what I'll make out of this one!'

'What one?'

'Who's having the last laugh now? I'm one step ahead of the authorities again, Rod, one step ahead.'

'What are you talking about, you nutter?'

Leon would always talk like this, in riddles.

'Come outside,' Leon replied.

Whenever Leon wanted to talk business, we would go for a walk, just in case his room was bugged. This kind of paranoid thinking goes with the territory when you're involved in the illegal drugs trade.

Once outside, he told me he had landed a haul of weed with a street value of more than half a million pounds.

I wasn't sure if he was telling me this just to see my reaction. I played it cool, but I couldn't stop thinking about the potential money I could make if he was telling the truth.

'Only you and Tony know, and it needs to stay that way,' Leon insisted.

'You know what I think about Tony. People are saying he's a grass. Be careful, mate.'

'I'm not stupid. Tony had to know, that's all I'm saying,' Leon replied.

'OK,' I said, biting my lip.

'I'll give you two kilos at a time,' Leon continued. 'You know the drill. You can have more once you've weighed in.'

This was music to my ears. By this time, I had stopped using weed so I knew I wouldn't be smoking away the profits myself. Plus, the price Leon was giving it to me at meant that I could lay it onto other people to sell for me and I would still make a tidy profit. This also lessened the risk of me getting caught by the police.

It was here that Lennie and Mickey came in useful. I knew they had a different circle of contacts from mine and both were happy to assist me in selling the 'merchandise'. They were, however, a mixed blessing.

When weighing in, Mickey was always on time, sometimes even paying up front for the next lot. He never let me down.

Lennie, on the other hand, was a nightmare. He would go quiet on me on 'payday'. He was a gambling addict like me so I should have known better. He would use my money and try to double it by betting on the football. When he lost, he would have to raise the money another way. Unlike Leon, I found it difficult to get aggressive and it wasn't like me to use threatening behaviour towards anyone who owed me money, even when it meant me being short when weighing in myself. Leon would tell me I was too soft. Maybe I just wasn't cut out for this game.

In order to keep a close eye on Lennie, I allowed him to stay at my house for a while. At least then he couldn't use any of his avoidance tactics. This was another unwise move. My house soon became the place to go for a party after the clubs had finished on weekends. My neighbours on this small, quiet cul-de-sac were not very appreciative of the noise we made and the music blaring out in the early hours of the morning. I became the neighbour from hell. On one occasion, a neighbour actually gatecrashed one of my parties and tried to swing his fist at me. Unfortunately, he ended up worse for wear when one of my friends jumped on him. My attempt at an apology the next time I saw him failed miserably. He wasn't having it. In fact, he got all the neighbours together one night to confront me about my behaviour and the disturbance and distress I was causing. They were completely right. I promised them that things would change. There was worse to come, though.

By this time, my old friends from college – Ponytail Dave, Charlie and Jamie – were all progressing well in life. Jamie had decided to go to university and the rest had really good jobs. As time had gone on and my life had become more and more chaotic, I saw less and less of them. I would sometimes have a drink with them if I saw them out in a pub, but that was about it. Dave was actually very wary of Leon, and I could tell he was concerned about my involvement with him. How things had changed from my college days!

Hannah and I would still speak on the phone, but it wasn't like it used to be. Our relationship had become very strained. The only time I really saw her was if she and her boyfriend had fallen out. She would normally come round to my house if I was in and we would watch a movie – usually Notting Hill. We both found the Welsh bloke in it hilarious. These few occasions were probably the only moments of normality I had.

I eventually kicked Lennie out of my house as he wasn't making any headway in getting me the money he owed me. My home soon became a bit of a dosshouse. I had all sorts of people staying, including two lads who were from Manchester, Mark and Joel. I had met them through mutual friends.

They were younger than me but seemed sound enough. Mark was quite short, with tanned skin, black wavy hair and big sideburns. He had a disgusting habit of picking his nose and spitting every five minutes. Joel was about five foot ten, with blonde shaven hair and a baby face.

Mark and Joel had been friends for years. Mark had fled to Guernsey because of a drugs debt. He had some money, so, unlike Lennie, was able to pay me rent. I was happy with that. Joel seemed to look up to Mark and would do anything for him.

I had sussed that Mark was up to something and that there was a reason Joel was with him. Mark told me that he was in debt to the tune of about £20,000 and that his family would be hurt if he didn't sort the money out.

We had something in common, as I was also in debt to Leon. It was only a few thousand pounds, but it was still money I didn't have.

In order to pay off our debts, our two criminal minds hatched a plan to import a batch of Ecstasy tablets. We had a contact in London who could get them for £1 a pill if we bought a thousand. Mark was to go to London to sort the deal, while Joel stayed with me. Joel would take delivery of the pills on their arrival in Guernsey. He would get a cut for taking such a big risk. That was the plan, anyway.

A few days before Mark went to London, I noticed that he was acting quite oddly and was being very secretive. He would frequently go up to his bedroom and then come down looking completely wasted – which I initially thought was because he had smoked a joint. When I talked to him he would suddenly drop off, as if sleeping, then regain consciousness. I also noticed he was scratching himself a lot, and what looked like a red rash appeared between his nose and mouth.

'What you been up to, Mark? Tell me. You're off your trolley.'

'Just a bit of brown, Hot Rod,' he replied. 'I didn't really want you to know.'

'You mean heroin?'

'Yeah. I ain't had it for a while. It's just nice to have a toot[1] every now and then.'

'How did you get hold of it?'

'I bumped into an old friend in town I knew back home. He's over for a week. He gave me some.'

'You look like you're on another planet. What's the buzz like?'

'It's completely different from anything you'd have experienced before, Hot Rod. It makes you feel nice and relaxed and very chilled. It's like you enter into your own little world where everything is OK – a world where all your problems disappear.'

'Have you got any left?' I asked.

'I have, but I didn't want to offer you any as it's very addictive. That's why I kept it quiet.'

'I'll be OK. Go on, give us a go.'

Up until then, I had never had anything to do with heroin. I had never even seen it, and I didn't know it was available in Guernsey. The closest I had ever come to the drug was when watching the movie *Trainspotting*. You'd think that watching a very graphic portrayal of people's lives being destroyed by heroin addiction would be enough to put someone off trying what's sometimes called the 'devil's poison'.

But no.

---

[1] A term used for smoking heroin.

For me, this was the next step on the destructive path I was already on, chasing the next high. In this case, I was chasing the dragon.

'Chasing the dragon' is a term used for smoking heroin on tin foil. This is done by placing the brown powder on the foil and heating it below with a lighter. The heroin then turns to a sticky liquid and wiggles around like a Chinese dragon, hence the name. Fumes are given off and inhaled through a rolled-up tube, usually made of foil. This was the way Mark had been using the substance.

I went upstairs with Mark to his room. He opened the drawer next to his bed and pulled out a small piece of tin foil. There was some heroin still left on it.

'Are you sure you want to do this, Hot Rod? It may make you feel sick.'

'Yeah, I'm sure. It's my choice, mate.'

Mark handed me the tube and told me to follow the liquid, inhaling the smoke at the same time.

I did as he said.

After a few seconds, I let out the smoke. My stomach immediately felt queasy. '*I'm going to be sick!*' I shouted.

I ran straight to the toilet and vomited everywhere.

'I did warn you,' Mark said, smiling.

I sat down in the lounge. Although I had just been sick, I did feel quite relaxed. I wasn't as wasted as I thought I would be because I had only smoked a little, and all the vomiting had removed some of the edge.

The next day, after I had finished work, I decided to give it another go. This time, I managed to stop myself from being sick. I also had more than the last time.

Mark was right. It was like nothing I had experienced before. It felt good, really good.

Every time I closed my eyes I had the most surreal dreams, even though I wasn't asleep. This is known as 'gauching'. I didn't have a care in the world. I didn't want this feeling to end.

I had heard people describe the effects of heroin as like being wrapped up in a cotton-wool bubble. I couldn't have described it better.

But I had no inkling of how much destruction this brown powder would unleash on my life and the people around me.

7.

Taking the Crazy Drug

When I started using heroin, I opened the gates of hell.

It was a Sunday afternoon, only two days after Mark had left for London. He was due to be away for a week. Joel and I had been out on the town the night before, and as usual a few people had come back to my house for a party. This included Mel and Rachel. The four of us were planning on going out to get something to eat.

I was in the bathroom getting ready when I heard the front door open and slam shut. The next thing I heard was screaming coming from the living room. I shot into the lounge and saw the girls holding each other and crying. There were two men I didn't recognize standing over Joel, shouting.

'Where's the filthy little rat?'

'I don't know,' Joel cried.

One of Joel's eyes was already looking puffed and swollen where they had hit him.

'What's going on?' I yelled.

The two men, who looked to be in their mid-twenties, were both wearing jeans, zip-up sports jackets and baseball caps. They had Mancunian accents. They turned to me with a look that implied 'Don't try anything stupid'. I didn't intend to.

'You must be Hot Rod. Where's the smackhead you've been hiding?'

'Who are you talking about? I've not been hiding anyone.'

'We're talking about Mark. Now, where is he?' one of them shouted as he put his cigarette out on my living room floor, squashing it into the carpet with his trainer.

'He's gone off the island. What's the problem?'

They told me what I already knew. Mark had a big debt to pay. Leaving the island had probably saved his life. They wanted his blood.

They hadn't finished with Joel, though. They took him upstairs to his bedroom and beat him to a pulp. Joel's screams were deafening. In the midst of the chaos I couldn't help wondering what the neighbours must be thinking.

The two men eventually came downstairs, but they were still not satisfied. They continued to quiz me about Mark's whereabouts. I told them that he'd gone away on a 'business venture' (they both understood what that meant) and that if all went to plan they would get their money soon. They made me promise that I would let them know when Mark returned. I agreed – anything to get rid of them.

Rachel and Mel were in shock. So was I, to be honest. I couldn't believe what had just happened. We were thinking the worst when we went upstairs to see how Joel was. He was still alive, but looked as if he had been trampled under a stampede of wild horses.

From that moment I wanted Mark and Joel out of my house. I couldn't be doing with all this trouble, not with everything else that was going on. But we were in the middle of a deal. I couldn't pull out now.

I managed to get hold of Mark and told him what had happened. I could sense he was panicking.

'Don't tell them where I am! Promise me! I mean it! Don't tell them!'

'Well, sort the money out then, Mark. They said they'll be coming back.'

'I'm on it. Don't worry. By the end of the week it will all be sorted. You know the script.'

Joel was prepped to pick up the parcel containing the drugs. They were to be shipped to an address at the other end of the island. He would get a small cut for doing the dirty work. Mark and I would split the rest.

But things didn't go as planned. Joel got cold feet, so he arranged for somebody else – a good mate of mine, Terry – to pick it up instead. However, the police and customs were on to it. They intercepted the parcel and replaced it with a dummy package at the property. When Terry arrived to collect it, he was arrested.

When I heard the news, I was devastated. Terry was looking at six years in prison. It took me weeks to get my head round it. I felt guilty. I couldn't help but blame Mark and Joel, too. *If I had never met them, this would never have happened.* For once, it wasn't about the money any more. I didn't care. This was my mate's freedom being taken away from him.

Mark never returned from London and Joel soon left the island. My craving for heroin remained. I found out who had a supply on the island and bought some for my personal use.

I soon became acquainted with the few people who were using heroin at that time. Like me, they had only recently started using and experimenting with it. They thought they were in control, just as I did.

I first realized I had a problem when the supply of heroin on the island ran out. I would crave it like crazy and wouldn't be happy until I scored. At first, I could make 0.2 of a gram last me all day, smoking it on the foil. But over time I needed more. It wasn't cheap, either, not at Guernsey prices. At my worst I could spend anything between £200 and £300 a day on my addiction.

Leon had also started using heroin. As money was no object, whenever it was available he seemed to have an endless supply. If there was none on the island, users had no choice but to go 'cold turkey' and face the torment of withdrawing from the drug. I can only describe the symptoms as like having flu but ten times worse. It is a punishing experience that plays havoc with your mind and body. Over a period of three to five days there would be intense feelings of agitation, anxiety, muscle cramps, cold sweats, insomnia and, of course, severe cravings.

Heroin isn't a sociable drug. It doesn't make you want to go out. I stopped going to the pubs and clubs. That didn't appeal to me any more. I had no desire to take any other drug apart from heroin. My circle of friends changed, too. It was like being a member of a secret society whose activities were hidden from everyone else.

My addiction became so out of control that at work I would go into the toilet cubicle to have a 'toot' during the day. I would be at my desk 'gauching' while trying to process important transactions with my client's money. I would be so out of it that I couldn't think or act rationally.

On one occasion, when doing a foreign currency exchange, I made a huge error which cost the bank over £2,000. This was the beginning of the end as far as my job was concerned.

People began to notice my health deteriorating. I was losing weight rapidly. My family were becoming more and more worried about me, especially after my stepdad turned up at my house unplanned and saw the state of it. It had got so bad that you had to wipe your shoes on the way out.

Speaking of surprise visits, I'll never forget one particular hot July afternoon. Leon, Lennie and I were sitting in my living room. The curtains were shut as normal. Leon and I were smoking heroin. Lennie abstained; he avoided heroin, one of the very few drugs he did stay away from.

There was a knock on the door.

I wasn't expecting anyone. I went to the front door and looked to see who it was.

It was my dad.

I couldn't hide as he had clocked me.

'Dad, what are you doing here?'

'I've come to see how my son is doing.'

'Please don't come in,' I said sheepishly. But before I could finish, he had already walked in and gone straight into the living room.

Here's my dad's own account of his approach to the front door and what he felt when I opened it.

When I was a police officer, the raid would have taken place as follows: everyone would be ready – radios silent, no vehicles, dogs muzzled. The approach would be made on foot, with back doors and windows covered.

The front door would have been approached on my command. 'Go, go, go!'

That was then. This was now.

And now was very different.

By this point I had been retired a few years. It was a sunny afternoon in July. I was secretly on the Island of Guernsey and I was on my own, in civvies, and about to confront my son in his own home.

I was terrified about what I might find. Was Rod even there? How many were with him? Would it turn nasty?

I had heard a lot of things about one of the guys – not nice, not nice at all.

The previous day I had landed on the island and not told anyone I was there, not even my daughter, Emma, and her husband. I had stayed in a hotel room with a breathtaking view of the Channel, and I could see the coastline of France.

On any other day it would have been idyllic. But not today.

I had arranged to meet one of Rod's mates at a local park that morning. He turned up and we chatted a bit. The effects of substances on his life were written all over his face and in his eyes. Could I trust him? He seemed likeable enough, and after a few minutes I was convinced he actually felt compassion for me and Rod.

'You're right to be worried,' he said. 'I think Rod is totally off the rails. He's doing hard stuff. I'm concerned as well.'

I had sighed.

'If you want to catch him, come to his house this afternoon. He'll be doing heroin.'

My blood froze. I knew Rod was smoking, drinking, gambling and doing Es. But heroin? That was the last straw. It was going to stop today.

I approached the front door, recalling how eighteen months earlier I'd helped Rod move into his brand-new home. Now I was in fear and trepidation. I couldn't show it, though. Even if I was retired, I had to play the part of the police inspector.

I tapped the glass in the door and waited.

Suddenly a figure appeared, and the door opened wide. It was my son.

His face went ashen and he looked stunned.

'Oh Dad, please don't come in,' he whimpered. As he spoke, I noticed that his teeth were covered in brown residue from that hellish drug, heroin.

I ignored Rod's request.

I walked straight in and was confronted by a scene reminiscent of every drug den I'd ever raided. There was a terrible smell of burning and drugs. There was a clutter of furniture, and the kitchen was dirty and trashed. The lounge looked as if it had been raided or burgled.

I felt anger, pity, nausea – but also, somehow, a feeling that this was going to be the beginning of the end in some way.

Did I call the police?

No.

Did I give the men in the house a kicking?

No.

I warned all three that what they were doing was not only illegal but could result in a long prison sentence. I reminded them of the destructiveness and devastation that this would have on their lives if they continued, and of how much our family was being destroyed because of Rod's actions.

I summed it up by saying this: 'Listen, you three will end up either dead, in prison or in hospital – that's the truth.' This was almost prophetic.

I did offer all three help if they wanted it, but I then had to leave them to make the choice for themselves.

I left after about an hour. My mind was fried. It was about the worst thing a police officer father could find: a son who was destroying his home, his life and his family – and for what? A few moments of illegal highs.

This was my son.

The little lad I had played with, nursed, and taken to school.

Despite what my dad saw, he appeared to me to be surprisingly calm. He sat down in the living room and asked the three of us to stay as he wanted to talk to us. Leon was reluctant, but agreed. My dad challenged us that afternoon to stop what we were doing. He had seen countless people's lives end in tragedy during his thirty years in the force. Why would we be any different? He suggested that we should enrol on a residential drug-rehab programme, one that had a Christian ethos and a proven success rate. He said it would be hard, but it would change our lives. We all listened. I said very little. What he said was true, but was I ready to give up this lifestyle?

Lennie encouraged me to listen to my dad's advice. He had seen my life deteriorate rapidly since I'd started taking heroin.

Leon thought my dad was just interfering. Even if I wanted to opt out, I still owed Leon money, and he wouldn't let it go that easily. The only way I was going to pay it off was to take on more weed to sell. So I did. I decided to try to get the debt paid as soon as possible. He was getting impatient.

However, there was one course of action which could sort things out fast – selling my house. I had been living there for almost two years and house prices had risen considerably. I worked out that I was in £30,000 of debt altogether – this included family debts, credit card debts, loans and the money I owed Leon. I could make this on the sale of the house, so I put it on the market. It was a good job I did because not long after that I quit my job at the bank. I didn't really have much of a choice as I was on the verge of being sacked anyway. Towards the end I was regularly phoning in sick. Even when I was there, I wasn't productive because my head was always mashed.

The house sold within a couple of months. The money was paid straight into my stepdad's bank account. He took what was owed him and also cleared my debts with my creditors. It felt good not having those hanging over my head. I was able to pay Leon some of the debt and I planned to pay him the rest from money I was owed myself.

Surely now I would be able to sort my life out.

How wrong I was.

After a brief spell living with my mum and stepdad, I decided to move in with a friend who lived with his mum. They had a big house so I rented one of the rooms. This wasn't the wisest move as my friend was also a heroin user. In fact, he had been using it longer than me and had started injecting the drug as well as smoking it. He would go into the bathroom to 'shoot up' (inject), thinking I didn't know what he was doing. Having a fear of needles was probably a good thing, as that put me off taking heroin this way. But even so we would stay up the best part of the night getting wasted.

In October 2001, Lennie invited me to go out for my birthday along with some other friends. It had been a while since I had been around town, so I agreed to go as a one-off. We had only been in one pub and were about to head to another when somebody in a drunken state who was standing in the doorway started shouting abuse at me. He then threw a punch at me. I managed to duck and followed through with some punches myself, and we got into a scuffle. The police appeared out of nowhere, pulled us apart and placed us under arrest. I was handcuffed and put into the back of a nearby police car.

As I was waiting to be taken to the police station, things escalated outside the pub. Protesting my innocence, Lennie and everybody else who was out with us also got arrested for disorderly conduct.

While all this was going on, I escaped out of my handcuffs. This was quickly spotted by a female police officer, who alerted her colleagues. I wasn't planning on doing anything but was just messing around. However, the officers didn't find it amusing and I was dragged from the back seat of the car face down onto the cold hard concrete ground outside. We were all taken to the holding cells at the station and kept there overnight. The next day, we were released pending further investigation, but were later charged with disorderly behaviour.

Weeks later, I bumped into one of the arresting officers, who pulled me to one side. Smiling, he said, 'Go on, Rodric, tell me how you got out of those handcuffs.'

'It's a trade secret,' I replied.

'You've got us all baffled,' he added.

That stunt led to me being known as an escapologist. This was even entered onto my police file.

Even though this had been a minor incident, it still meant going to court again and getting another conviction. I needed to get off the island.

A mate of mine called Jocko had decided to leave the island too. He had booked a one-way ticket to Thailand, leaving in December. He had a mate out there, called Moose, who owned his own bar.

'Come out with me, Hot Rod! Let's get away from all of this! It's not doing either of us any good being here.'

'How much money will I need?'

'Three grand. That should last you six months over there, including your ticket.'

I made my mind up. I was going. This was going to be it. No more gambling, no more heroin, no more dealing. I genuinely believed this was what I needed to sort my head out.

My ticket was booked and I was excited. My family were not as thrilled, though. To them, I couldn't have picked a worse place to go. Some areas of Thailand are described like a modern-day Sodom and Gomorrah. Need I say more?

We arrived in Bangkok mid-December and spent Christmas in the city of Pattaya, staying in a hotel that was on the same street as Moose's bar. Moose, also from Guernsey, had lived there for a number of years, having set up the business with his mum. There were other Guernsey folk visiting too; they were there for the wild non-stop partying night life.

I had not used heroin for two weeks but was drinking heavily instead. Jocko was a twenty-stone beer monster and was rarely seen without a bottle in his hand. I tried to keep up with him.

If I thought that getting away was going to mean conquering my addictions, I was completely wrong. It was during this time that I was introduced to a small red tablet called Yaba. Made up of methamphetamine and caffeine, it can be taken orally or chased on foil like heroin.

Methamphetamine is a highly addictive drug that causes the brain to flood with a substance called dopamine, causing huge exhilaration at first but then terrible lows. Even low levels of abuse can cause clinical depression and psychosis.

Yaba translates as 'crazy drug'. After witnessing first-hand the mental state of some who were regular users, I realized that couldn't have been a truer description. Yet this didn't stop me taking Yaba constantly for three weeks. As the drug is a form of speed, users can be awake for days at a time. Yaba was originally invented by the Nazis, who created the stimulant to keep the troops awake for days during the Second World War. Having no or very little sleep was something I found hard to cope with. My mind was all over the place, and so were my emotions. For no apparent reason I would start crying in public and would be unable to control myself. I must have looked a right headcase. To help with the comedown, I found a dodgy chemist who sold me Valium and morphine-based painkillers from under the counter.

Having an unlimited supply of these downers (tranquillizers), I would eat them like sweets. This meant that I lasted only six weeks out of my planned six months in Thailand, because I ran out of money a lot more quickly than expected.

A couple of days before I was due to leave Thailand, there was a phone call for me at the bar. It was Leon.

'Hi, mate. What's up?' I asked.

'You know what's up. Did you think I wouldn't notice?'

'Notice what?'

'Sixty grand, that's what! Tell me the truth. You know something about it?'

Leon told me that someone had robbed £60,000 worth of weed from his stash. He was upset. Very upset.

'I told you not to trust Tony. It's obvious it's him. I'm back in a couple of days. We can talk then.'

That was all I needed, going back to this kind of trouble.

Even so, I packed my bags to go home. Moose and Jocko threw a leaving party for me and invited all the regulars, some of whom I'd got to know quite well. Jocko had no intention of returning with me. He and Moose were planning on leaving Pattaya to set up a hotel business on the island of Ko Samui. I told them I would return as soon as I could.

On returning home I was met by my family. I went straight back to my mum and stepdad's house, where I had decided to stay. It was good to see them. I put on my 'everything's OK' mask, but they knew different.

The cravings started almost immediately. Within hours of returning I was using heroin again. Leon also caught up with me. He told me in more detail what had happened, looking intensely at me to gauge my reaction. He got Tony and me together and threatened to throw sulphuric acid over us if one of us didn't own up to stealing the stash. Neither of us did. Even if I had done it, there was no way I would have admitted to it.

Not long after this, Tony fled the island. This took the heat off me. For a while, anyway.

Fed up of paying the high prices for heroin in Guernsey, I decided to go to London for a few days. I knew I could score there at a fraction of the price. I ended up in Brixton and soon made contact with the wrong sorts. I got my fix of brown and also tried crack cocaine. This was also extremely addictive.

I had a contact who lived in a house just up the road from Brixton Tube station. Actually, it was more of a squat – a crack den, even. I ended up staying there myself, along with other addicts. The few days turned into two weeks. It was a very dark fortnight. I was surrounded by crooks, dealers and messed-up addicts. I was popular because I had money and was very generous sharing my gear.

By my own admission I wasn't exactly the most streetwise person. One afternoon, I went into a betting shop just down the road from the squat. I had £2,000 on me in twenties. This was a sum I had just had put into my bank account by a friend in Guernsey. I promised to pay him back with interest within a week. The money was meant to fund my new addiction to crack cocaine. Every time I placed a bet I would pull out the pile of notes, never suspecting that I was being watched. After losing a few hundred pounds I left, and in broad daylight made my way back to the squat.

Before I knew it, two black guys jumped on me and went straight for the pocket where the money was and ran off. I had been robbed. How could I have been so stupid? I went back to the squat with nothing, not one single penny.

My head was banging. Perhaps this wasn't really happening and I would wake up and find it had all just been a dream. Well, I did wake up, but only after falling asleep on a filthy floor, using a black rubbish bag as a pillow. When I woke I stood up and looked around the room. There were sleeping bodies everywhere. The grimy floor was covered with used needles and the paraphernalia of drug addiction. Blood, urine and vomit stained the carpet. The stench was horrific.

Surrounded by squalor, my tears began to fall.

How did I ever end up here?

I remembered moments from my happy childhood. I thought of my loving family and their warm and welcoming home, and my good friends whom I had let down. Through my own choices I had ended up penniless, in a dirty squat filled with the thickest darkness. I had to get away, even if it meant swallowing my pride.

I phoned my dad in Wales and asked him to help me. He said he would, and got me on the next train. I had no drugs or medication to help with my withdrawals. I had to go cold turkey again. I barely got out of bed for five days.

After many more challenging talks from my dad, I promised him that I would put an end to this lifestyle once and for all. He took me for an interview at a nearby Christian rehab centre. Their verdict was that I hadn't reached rock bottom. I therefore wasn't ready to join the programme yet.

My dad was discouraged by this but he didn't give up hope. He and I wrote down a twelve-month action plan that looked promising on paper.

It didn't quite work out in practice.

The plan was for me to go back to Guernsey to stay with my family and keep my head down. Surprise, surprise, I started using heroin again. I then met up with a friend of mine, Joanne, who I knew was interested in going to Thailand to visit her friends in Ko Samui. As that was where Jocko and Moose were planning to move to, we agreed to go together. We both booked an open return ticket and were due to leave in a few weeks (Friday, 15 March 2002). We spent a lot of time together during those weeks. I must admit that I probably wasn't the best of influences on her, but we both thought this trip would do us good and we vowed to make a completely fresh start upon our return. I'd lost count of how many times I'd said that before.

I told Leon my plan to go back to Thailand, that I was serious this time in wanting to sort my head out, and that I wanted out of this criminal life. I could tell he didn't like it. He told me I still owed him eight grand. I disagreed, but there was no negotiating with Leon when it came to money. I could also tell he was still very angry about not getting to the bottom of his stolen stash of weed. It was only a matter of time before Leon flipped.

It was exactly one week before Joanne and I were to go to Thailand. It was a Friday, and I had planned to stay in with my family for the first time in ages. Leon, however, had other ideas. He came to my mum and stepdad's house and insisted I went out with him. I had no choice. He took me to his basement flat, where he threatened me and said he intended to hurt my family if I didn't pay up. He gave me one week to pay the remaining debt.

I knew I couldn't get that kind of money in such a short space of time, so I made the decision to do one last deal. Through the contacts I had made in London, I knew I could get whatever I wanted at a good price.

The next night I decided to go out and meet Mickey and Joanne for a drink down at the Harbour Lights pub. On my way I bumped into Hannah, whom I hadn't seen in a while. She wasn't very encouraging.

'Look at the state of you – you look awful! And the people you hang around with! What are you doing with your life?'

'I'm trying, Hannah, I really am. I'm sorry for letting you down,' I replied.

'You're on that stuff. I don't understand why. I just can't get my head round it, Hot Rod. You were such a good friend. Look at you now. Sort yourself out before it's too late.'

I could see how genuinely upset she was. The truth hurt me. It went deep. I didn't deserve her as a friend.

I went into the pub and told Mickey and Joanne what had gone on with Leon. Joanne was concerned and told me not to do anything stupid. She was so looking forward to getting away. So was I. Chatting with Mickey afterwards, I told him how my life was tearing me apart and that I wanted out. Mickey felt exactly the same. That night, he also talked seriously about stopping and making a fresh start.

'I've just got to do one more thing, Hot Rod, then I'm done with it all. Why don't you come in with me? You'll be able to get Leon off your back.'

'I can't. I need to sort my situation out quickly, over the next few days.'

'Be careful, Rod. You're a good mate. You're different from the rest.'

'You too, Mickey. We can do this.'

We both went our separate ways: me to do my thing, and he to do his.

Our worlds would soon collide again, however, in a way we did not expect.

8.

A Make-or-Break Deal

'I'm prescribing you diazepam and zopiclone,'[2] my doctor said after examining me first thing on the Monday morning. It was three days after my ordeal with Leon. There were only five days to go before I left for Thailand.

I had woken up that day with a profound feeling of stress and the beginnings of an anxiety attack, all brought on by the situation with Leon and my craving for heroin.

Having been to the doctor and collected my meds, I then went round to the house of a friend called Craig, also known as 'Crazy'. He had earned this nickname on account of his unpredictable and temperamental behaviour. Whatever the time of day or night, Crazy was always ready to do something mad.

Crazy was of mixed race, was short, of average build, and had spiky black hair. He was unemployed at the time, but managed to make ends meet by ripping people off in drugs deals. On one occasion, I remember him selling someone a line of Polyfilla, claiming it was speed. On another, he sold someone a bag of crushed-down stinging nettles for £50, saying it was weed. I guess, in a way, he was right. Stinging nettles are a kind of weed.

---

[2] Sleeping tablets.

Crazy's front door was always open, so I walked straight in and climbed the stairs to his bedroom, where I found him on his mixing decks playing old school rave tunes.

'Fancy sharing these?' I said, holding out the drugs the doctor had prescribed.

Crazy didn't need to answer. I pulled out the blister packs, divided the pills in half, and the two of us downed the lot before heading to the local pub to drink a few pints. In no time at all we were off our heads, playing pool and betting on the horses. I felt no anxiety. My confidence was sky high. I wasn't afraid of anything or anyone. I felt totally invincible.

As I told Crazy about my dilemma with Leon, a plan began to form in my head.

'Do you fancy a trip to London for the night?' I asked. 'I'm paying. We can get some gear and have a final blast before I leave for Thailand.'

'You know me, Hot Rod, always up for a mad one!' Crazy replied.

'I also need to sort out a big debt,' I added.

'No problem!'

By 3 p.m. we had driven to the airport.

'The next flight is at 5.15 p.m.,' I said. 'I'm going to need to book us back on the 8 a.m. flight tomorrow morning.'

'Why that early?' Crazy moaned.

'I'm due in court at 10 a.m.'

'What for?'

'Disorderly conduct.'

Crazy laughed his head off.

I paid the £500 for the two return flights, never considering for a moment that two young men embarking on a fifteen-hour trip from the island might look dodgy. Neither of us was thinking straight, and it never occurred to us that the suspicions of Guernsey's Special Branch might be aroused or that they might clock our movements. Having said that, I was conscious enough to realize that we might need a reason for our visit, so I drove us to the house of our friend Bonehead, where we borrowed his DJ bag and some records. When I say 'borrowed', I really mean 'stole'. Bonehead wasn't in, so we broke in and took his stuff. He only lived round the corner from the airport.

'If anyone asks,' I said to Crazy as we drove back to the airport, 'we're going to DJ in a club in London. That's our story.'

We boarded the flight to Gatwick and within minutes we were up and away, pumped with excitement, knowing that very soon our cravings for heroin and crack cocaine would be satisfied. I felt I was holding the winning lottery ticket and I was on my way to collect a fortune.

We landed and made our way to the Gatwick Express, then on to the Tube to Brixton. After a quick taxi ride, we arrived at the flat of a contact I'd made on my last visit a few weeks earlier. He was a white guy in his forties called Gadget and seemed trustworthy. His flat was smart and kitted out with all the latest appliances and gadgets, hence his nickname. This was the Ritz compared with where I had stayed on my last visit.

'Gadget, look, I need some gear and I need it fast. If you can sort it, you can have a night on us.'

I had already worked out that if I bought twenty-eight grams of heroin and fourteen grams of crack cocaine, it would cost me around £1,500. Even with the three of us getting smashed from an all-night session, I reckoned that I'd still have more than enough to make the £8,000 I needed to pay off my debt.

Gadget made a call to his supplier and within minutes we had a couple of rocks of crack to get us started. Gadget had his crack pipe ready and I inhaled the first rock. An intense euphoria hit me like a ton of bricks. It felt amazing, but it wore off quickly, leaving me wanting more.

I told Gadget's supplier exactly how much I needed.

'We'll have to go elsewhere for that amount,' he said. 'I know where to find it, but you'll have to come with me.' He never did tell me his name.

Crazy decided to stay at Gadget's flat, so I was now out in the dark streets of London being driven in unfamiliar territory to pick up the gear with a solidly built Jamaican man with dreadlocks whom I had met only minutes earlier. I don't mind admitting it: I was scared.

He picked up a mate of his and we continued to drive for what seemed like hours.

I was really nervous now.

There was £1,500 in my wallet. *What if they mug me, take the money and leave me for dead?*

My drug-induced paranoia increased as the car stopped outside a block of flats and the two men got out.

'We'll be back soon – get your money ready,' one of them whispered, leaning through the window.

I was left in the freezing cold and pitch darkness for a good hour. *What if I get killed out here and my family never find my body?*

To my relief, they eventually returned.

'Here,' one of them said, passing me the drugs. 'It's not as much as you wanted because there's a shortage of brown; it's never been so bad. After my cut, there'll be about a quarter ounce of brown and about three quarters of crack.'

I was relieved. I was OK, and I had the drugs.

Although it wasn't exactly what I'd asked for, it was still enough to make a large profit at Guernsey prices.

After another long drive, we returned to Gadget's place, where he was waiting at the entrance to the block of flats.

I asked the driver if he would pick us up at 6 a.m. and drop us off at the airport. He said he would, for some cash. That wasn't a problem – as long as we got there.

'I thought you'd been killed!' Crazy stammered when I returned to the flat with Gadget.

Although he was concerned, all that quickly disappeared when I loaded up the crack pipe. It was only fair for me to do a tester. It hit the spot nicely. I couldn't move for a couple of minutes. I thought my head was going to explode. This was good gear.

'This is the plan,' I said to Crazy. 'We'll package the drugs in two birthday cards and post them to Guernsey as soon as we get to the airport.' I had already obtained all the materials to do this from a corner shop not far from Gadget's flat.

For the next few hours, the three of us engaged in a heavy session using both drugs. Before long, we had smoked almost half the crack I'd bought and most of the heroin – which was weaker than usual because of the shortage and because of how much of it had been 'bashed' (cut in order to dilute it). We tried to seal the remainder of the stash into small self-seal bags and tape them into the birthday cards, but they looked a complete mess. There was no way we were going to be able to use the services of Royal Mail to get the drugs to Guernsey. I couldn't afford to pay a courier to import them, either. My options were running out.

Or were they?

Although I had never done this before, I realized that I had no choice and that I was going to have to carry the drugs. I also figured that the police and customs officials wouldn't search me because they would never think I was stupid enough to do the dirty work myself.

So I made my decision, and I didn't let on about my intentions to either Gadget or Crazy. It was especially important for Crazy not to know because he would be a paranoid mess, due to the amount of crack he had smoked. So I made him think I was going ahead with the original plan.

In the end, our lift arrived half an hour late, so we had to rush to the airport. The driver had been up all night smoking the drugs he had made from the deal; he was very quiet and acting extremely strangely. As we headed towards Gatwick, he began to say that we weren't who we said we were, claiming that we were undercover policemen.

'We're not. You're just on a bad comedown, mate; you're paranoid,' I said nervously.

But the driver didn't believe me.

As his paranoia increased, his driving became more erratic. He began to swerve all over the roads, threatening to end it all. For the second time in less than four days I thought I was going to die. In the end, we managed to calm him down, but not before he had accused us again of setting him up. When we arrived at Gatwick, Crazy and I couldn't get out of the car and into the terminal quickly enough.

Crazy and I checked in and waited for our flight. There was just one hour before the plane took off, so we sat in the departure lounge.

I told Crazy I was going to look for a post box to post the cards, but I went instead to a sports store and purchased a brand-new pair of trainers. I then walked to the gents toilets and entered a cubicle. I removed my new trainers and socks, tore open the cards, and hid the drugs in their flattened packaging in the bottoms of my socks. I put these back on and then threw away the cards and their packaging as well as the old trainers.

I returned to Crazy, who was by this time completely out of it. He had no idea that the drugs were on me and had not been posted. As I looked at him, I began to feel anxious.

'Are you all right, mate?' I asked. 'You don't look well – not well at all.'

Crazy groaned, 'I'll be all right, Hot Rod.'

I sat with him in the lounge and decided to call Lennie. He was due in court with me that morning for the same offence.

'Lennie, can you be in the car waiting for me at the airport? I'll dash through customs straight out to you so we can leg it to court.'

'I'll be there,' he replied.

I put down the phone and heard the call for our flight.

As Crazy and I boarded the plane, I tried to look as calm as possible, but inside I was panicking. Crazy seemed to be getting worse, almost foaming at the mouth, and didn't seem to know where he was. Later, I learned that he'd smoked more drugs in the toilet at the airport.

All I could think of was getting through customs, selling the drugs and paying off my debt to Leon.

As the engines began to roar into action, I thought of my flight to Thailand, now just a matter of days away. I just wanted to jet off into the sunset and get away from it all. But this seemed worlds away right now.

To make matters even worse, I now discovered two cellophane-sealed rocks of crack cocaine in my pocket. That was all I needed.

I placed the rocks in my mouth and hid them under my tongue. This is common practice among street dealers. Not only does it conceal the stash, it also gives the dealer a chance to swallow it if confronted by police. I decided to adopt the same strategy.

Within minutes, the plane was approaching the island.

At last, I thought. *Ten minutes, and I'll be on the ground. Then I'm home and dry.*

But we didn't begin our descent. Instead, the plane began to circle the island for what seemed like half an hour.

Something was wrong. I knew it. But I tried to block the thought from entering my mind.

Is this the end?

My thoughts turned to my family.

What about Jo and Thailand?

My heart began to sink and I could feel the blood drain from my face. I had images racing through my head of customs officers, sniffer dogs, court rooms and prison.

Surely this was just paranoia.

9.

Bang to Rights

When the plane came to a halt at Guernsey Airport, it was obvious that the game was up. Through the windows of the cabin I could see familiar customs officers waiting outside. As soon as the door was opened, a dog rushed in and ran up and down the aisle, sniffing eagerly for the scent of drugs.

Everyone on board was asked to disembark and head to the arrivals hall. When I got there, I saw many more customs officers than usual. It seemed to me they had anticipated that this was going to be a big smuggling operation. I tried to act cool, calm and collected. I also put distance between myself and Crazy, who was now a dribbling mess.

I picked up my bag and tried to walk nonchalantly through customs, but it was no surprise when I was stopped and then escorted to a side room. Exactly the same thing happened to Crazy.

'Where have you been travelling to, sir?' an officer asked me.

'London.'

'What was the purpose of your visit?'

'I went for a night out at a club.'

'Are you aware that it is illegal to carry controlled substances on your person?'

'Yes, I am.'

I tried my best to talk my way through these routine questions as convincingly as I could. I even attempted to throw them off the scent by hinting to them that I thought Crazy might be carrying drugs. I was certain he wasn't, so, as far as I was concerned, I was not stitching him up. I was just getting them off my back.

However, these officers were not so easily distracted. For the next twenty minutes they continued to fire a salvo of questions at me. Eventually, they stopped their interrogation and tried a different tack.

'Are you willing to have a drugs test?' one of them asked.

'Yes,' I replied, before adding, 'I've been using opiates, cocaine and cannabis.'

Sure enough, the tests confirmed my confession, but my interrogators were not done yet.

They led me into another side room and told me they were going to conduct a strip search.

I realized I was fighting a losing battle, so halfway through the search I handed over the two packages that were concealed in the soles of my socks.

I will always remember this moment. My plan had failed, and yet an overwhelming sense of relief washed over me. I had been caught, yes, but this was what was needed for the chaotic and miserable life of drugs, addiction and crime I had been living to stop. There was no escaping my predicament, and in confronting that reality I felt glad.

For Crazy, of course, the situation couldn't have been more different. He was in another room and had absolutely no idea that the drugs had been found. As far as he was concerned, they were on their way to the island by Royal Mail. This was something of a comfort to me because I was well aware that he now couldn't be prosecuted for being 'knowingly concerned' and be charged for the same offence.

As soon as the drugs had been handed over, Crazy and I were each taken to the customs shed at St Peter Port Harbour, where we were held for further questioning and locked in separate rooms. I was clothed in a paper suit and put on a 24/7 watch. Those guarding me had to ensure that I was not concealing drugs internally in my body. This meant that every time I went to empty my bowels, I was watched by two officers, one of whom had the disgusting task of checking what I had just produced. The whole experience was degrading, both for them and for me.

I was also taken to a local hospital to be X-rayed to make sure there were no packages of drugs in my body. While I was being X-rayed, I still had the two crack rocks in my mouth, concealed under my tongue. Even after the X-rays and a mouth search, the officers didn't clock them.

Back in my room, I looked through the small glass panel in my door. There was always an officer observing me when I did this, but on one occasion I managed to look to one side of his face and caught a glimpse of Crazy walking past in his white paper suit. He cast a furtive glance towards my door. When he saw me, he gave me one of his cheeky grins. He still had no idea that I'd been caught with the drugs.

Later that afternoon, I was questioned by two officers. I stuck with my story about the London trip because Crazy and I had agreed on the details of this. I therefore had to go with it. The trouble was that the officers wanted detail.

'Where did you go? Why did you go there? Who did you go with? Who did you meet?'

I stuck with the story Crazy and I had concocted.

'We went to meet a mate who runs a nightclub. Crazy was the guest DJ and I was just there to support him and have a good time.'

'And who did you get the drugs from?'

'I don't know who it was – just somebody I met in the club.'

'Why did you buy them?'

'I'm an addict. I just bought them for my own personal use.'

'And did your friend know that you brought these drugs with you on the plane?'

'No, I can honestly say that he knows absolutely nothing about that.'

After more questioning I was led back to the holding room. A thousand thoughts were going through my head and I was an emotional wreck. The effects of the drugs had also worn off and I felt really rough. I had no cigarettes on me, but the duty customs officer gave me a half-full packet. He seemed like a nice guy.

That evening, a doctor was called out to examine me. He gave me a couple of sleeping tablets, which I swallowed. I felt less ill once they kicked in. Actually, I felt quite drunk, and they made me hallucinate slightly too.

In this mildly intoxicated state I suddenly thought it would be a good idea to remove one of the crack rocks from its package under my tongue. I lay on the hard mattress with a sheet over me, pretending to be asleep. I slowly unwrapped the rock which had been tightly enclosed in cellophane. I managed to swallow most of it.

This, however, left me with the cellophane. I couldn't swallow that, and I couldn't keep it, either. It was evidence. So I foolishly decided to hide it in the cigarette packet on the table in my cell. This was not the smartest move, given that I was being constantly watched through the window. In a flash, a custom's officer rushed through the door, followed quickly by several others. They found the cellophane, which still contained 0.04 grams of the drug. Panicking, I gulped down the other pellet under my tongue and it disappeared undiscovered into my stomach.

'Where did you get this?' one of the officers barked.

'It's been under my tongue the whole time,' I answered.

I'm not sure whether or not they believed me, but they left my cell after a thorough search, satisfied that there were no more packages.

The next morning, I woke up after just a few hours' sleep. It began to dawn on me what had just happened. The reality of what I had done, and what I was about to face, hit hard. Worst of all, I started to feel deep grief and guilt about the hurt my family would experience because of my actions.

At this stage I hadn't spoken to my family, but I knew they had found out because I was informed that my dad had been contacted just after my arrest. I envisioned the news headline – 'Ex-Police Inspector's Addict Son Remanded for Smuggling Offences'. What shame this would bring to my family who lived on the island. My stepdad had an excellent reputation, and now his address was going to be in the paper. If you only get a speeding conviction in Guernsey you get named and shamed. I decided I would give my address as 'no fixed abode' in court, as this wasn't far from the truth anyway.

I wanted to speak to Mum but I knew she would be devastated, so I couldn't bring myself to do it. I also couldn't bear to speak to Joanne because I knew that I had ruined all the plans for the Thailand trip. I did ask to make one phone call, however, and that was to my best friend, Hannah. I had always found her easy to talk to. She had seen me deteriorate over the years. Although I hadn't had much contact with her since starting taking heroin, I felt I needed to apologize to her.

'Hi, Hannah, it's me, Rod. Have you heard what's happened?'

'Yes, Rod – it was on the radio this morning that you'd been arrested. Is it true?'

'Yes, I'm afraid it is, Han.'

'Oh, Hot Rod, enough is enough,' she sighed. I could hear the disappointment in her voice. 'You can't keep doing this any more. Think about what you're doing to your poor family.'

I couldn't deny it. I had put my family through hell, and Hannah's words hit hard.

'I'm sorry, Hannah.'

I asked her if she would contact Joanne to tell her what had happened and that I would not be going to Thailand. 'And please tell her how sorry I am.'

'I will – and let me know when I can visit you.'

This is the right moment to let Hannah share all this from her perspective. Here are her reflections about what was happening to me at this time.

Rod and I first met in our late teens and became very close friends. We hit it off from the start, having similar interests and sharing the same sense of humour. I could see he was a nice, kind and gentle person and had been brought up well by his family, who were also genuine, kind-hearted people. I enjoyed his company.

Back in those early days, a group of us would go out most evenings in Rod's red Ford Fiesta. There was a pub we all liked to go to along the coast at Vazon. We would normally spend a couple of hours in there, have a couple of drinks and then go for a drive around the island.

Rod and I would go everywhere together, often going tenpin bowling or to watch the latest film at the cinema. Even after I had met my boyfriend, this didn't change. Rod and I were like family, in a strange kind of way.

At weekends we would meet up and go into town with friends for a few drinks and then off to a nightclub. I have a lot of good memories from these times. We were young and just having fun. 'Hot Rod' very quickly became popular with everybody. He was always introducing me to new people he had met, some of whom I knew were not going to be a good influence because of their bad reputation. I began to question Rod's activities. He began to change for the worse.

He started to sell Ecstasy pills in the clubs. I could see he was relishing every bit of his new-found popularity. Rod liked flashing the cash and was always buying rounds of drinks for everybody. I knew he was doing this because of the money, but I could never understand why, because he had a good job and was earning more money than I could ever see myself earning.

Even though I didn't want to acknowledge it, I knew one day this would all end in disaster.

One thing I will always say is that Rod would never willingly turn his back on his real friends. It was his poor choices and the people he associated with who opened the door to a scene I didn't want to participate in. This meant that I saw less and less of Rod. When I did see him, it was obvious from his appearance and the way he would act that he was deteriorating. He would chain-smoke and struggle to string a sentence together. He looked dreadful. I later found out that he was using heroin.

I could hardly believe it. Nobody who knew Rod could believe it either. There was no telling him, though. He had no idea where this path was going to take him.

Rod would never admit this to me, despite the many times I challenged him. In fact, he told me so many lies, but even then I would still defend him to others. I didn't think Rod would ever lie to me. It hurt.

I tried to understand why he was doing what he was doing, but I couldn't. Maybe if he had admitted his addiction to heroin to his real friends, things might have been different. We might have been able to help. Deep down, I felt this would have a very bad ending – visiting Rod in prison or, worse still, at his graveside.

One day, in March 2002, I received a phone call from Rod telling me that he had been arrested for drug importation and was looking at a long prison sentence. I was upset – even angry – that he hadn't listened to me, but at the same time I was relieved because I believed this would probably save his life. It was common knowledge *that Guernsey prison was different from others and that drugs were very hard to get inside, especially heroin, so this was a good opportunity for Rod to get clean.*

Having a close friend go down the destructive path of addiction, then seeing them inside a prison, was extremely upsetting. I felt crushed inside. I remember feeling very tearful and disappointed the first time I visited Rod in prison – maybe even guilty: 'Did I give up on him?'

Fortunately, Rod is still alive to tell his story.

Unfortunately, this is not the case for so many others who decide to take the same path in life.

After I had finished my phone conversation with Hannah, I was taken to an interview room. I was questioned a second time and then formally charged on two counts for the importation of a controlled substance. I was informed that I'd be escorted to a police station later that day and then to court the following morning.

I asked for a pen and some paper and began to write letters to my family, saying sorry for what I had done and for all that I'd put them through. As I scribbled, tears poured down my cheeks onto the paper. I couldn't run away from what I had done, and the consequences of my actions were now inescapable. The people who cared for me the most, who had offered their love and support when most would have given up, were the ones who were going to be hurt the most.

That afternoon, Crazy and I were taken in separate vehicles to the police station, where we were held overnight. I saw a duty lawyer, who talked me through what I was to expect and told me that I'd be remanded in custody to await sentencing at the Royal Court. I was told the exact quantity of drugs I had been charged with carrying, which turned out to be less than I thought – 10.5 grams of crack cocaine and just under 2 grams of heroin. This was small enough to make me think that I would get away with it being classed as personal use.

The next morning, Crazy and I were put in the back of the court police van. This was the first time we had been together since our arrest. He looked really rough. Surprisingly, I didn't feel that bad.

'Crazy, I had the drugs on me. I'm in court for importation of class A drugs.'

'But I thought you'd posted them!' he replied with astonishment.

'I'm sorry, mate, I didn't. I had them on me all the time.'

'You're joking!'

'I'm not.'

Slowly, I could see the lights coming on in Crazy's head.

'I thought the officers were just blagging when they said they'd found drugs on you,' he said. 'It all makes sense now.' After a moment, he added, 'Hot Rod, you're mental! Why did you do that?'

'You saw the mess we made with the packages. I didn't want to take the risk of them being opened and discovered. I had no choice.'

'Well, I guess I'm not one to talk,' Crazy said. 'Turns out I was carrying 0.2 grams of crack. I've been charged too.'

In the magistrate's court, Crazy and I were remanded in custody for one week. This was the norm, but I had no doubts that in a week's time I would be remanded once again. Even though we had reserved our plea, I realized that pleading 'not guilty' was not an option.

I was bang to rights and heading for prison.

10.

Freed on the Inside

As two prison officers escorted Crazy and me straight from the court to the prison van, I don't mind admitting I was nervous. I had never been to prison before, other than to visit mates. I had no idea what to expect and I was experiencing very mixed emotions. On the one hand, I was pleased that I was about to be reunited after a long time with old mates who'd been sent down for crimes similar to mine. On the other hand, prison seemed like another world compared with anything I had been used to, and I was apprehensive.

My foundations were shifting like tectonic plates.

Crazy and I sat with our hands cuffed in the back of the prison van. The journey from court to Les Nicolles Prison didn't take long – about fifteen minutes.

In the van with us was a young guy called Ollie. He had been remanded in custody for importing Ecstasy tablets. He was looking at six years. It was evident by his facial expression that he was finding it tough. Ollie became a good mate of mine.

The van slowed and came to a halt at a massive steel prison gate which lifted slowly after we had checked in. We drove into an inner yard and got out of the van. The buildings looked cold, oppressive and hostile, like a run-down and sinister-looking school.

Everywhere I looked I couldn't help noticing the high level of security. Everything was behind bars. There were imposing fences, coils of razor wire, spotlights and closed-circuit cameras. There was no way out.

This was a place that exuded authority and demanded cooperation. After living a chaotic lifestyle with no structure or boundaries, I knew that this place would be the complete opposite. My life was about to change radically.

Although I was 24 years old, at that moment I felt like a vulnerable, frightened child. There were no words of comfort or shoulders to cry on. The process of induction was conducted in a clinical, matter-of-fact manner. There was no coffee offered and no magazines provided to read while you waited, just the grim humiliation of being strip-searched once again by uniformed strangers.

After being searched, I was handed a black bin sack containing the only items that I was now permitted to have: a pale blue plastic plate, bowl and beaker, with cutlery to match, and two sets of prison-issue clothing, consisting of grey joggers, a pale blue T-shirt and a burgundy sweatshirt. It was like I was back at nursery school.

With the induction over, two prison officers came to escort me to my double cell on F-wing. As I walked along the corridors, adrenalin began to pump around my body, swamping and heightening my senses. Every colour seemed more vivid, especially the bright green of the bars and heavy metal doors. I was hyper-sensitive to sounds punctuating the air – the banging of metal, the rattling of keys and the squeaking of shoes. Voices boomed from every space. Intense smells assaulted my nostrils – especially the odour of disinfectant and floor polish, which seemed to stick to the back of my throat.

Such were the sights, sounds and smells that hit me on my first day. They were to be my constant companions for the next two years, alongside a feeling of degradation which on my first day almost overcame me.

I soon arrived on F-wing, which was smaller than I had imagined. In fact, Les Nicolles, the only prison on Guernsey, is very small compared with others, with capacity for 122 prisoners; at this time there were only 54.

F-wing had eleven cells, and it was 'bang up' time, so most of the prisoners were behind closed doors, apart from a few familiar faces on 'enhanced level' who had just returned from working in the kitchen. Three of our old mates, Flaxy, Martyn and Venu, greeted Crazy and me. They were also inside for drugs-related offences. When they saw us, they shouted to all the other prisoners who were locked in their cells, 'Hot Rod and Crazy are in, lads!'

At this, someone else shouted out, 'Do your bird, Hot Rod!'

I'm not sure I was amused by this remark which means 'do your time' – the bird being a reference to being locked up in a cage – but it was meant with good humour.

Crazy and I were now shown to our cell and given some time to clean it. We were then locked up until evening meal time and association – time out of the cells for recreational activities such as using the gym or library, or playing pool or table tennis.

The cell was stark and sterile. Harsh metal bunk beds stood against one wall, complete with blocks of foam covered in blue plastic which did for mattresses. Just an arm's length away, a wooden desk and wardrobe furnished the opposite wall. The floor was cold and shiny. The only natural light came from a small window dominated by forbidding metal bars.

The cell communicated a wordless message of punishment and deprivation. To my surprise – and relief – there was a separate, albeit tiny, room with a toilet and sink. This was because it was classed as a double cell, although single cells could also be doubled up if space was short.

Crazy and I sat down and rolled up a cigarette using some tobacco that Flaxy had given us. It still really hadn't sunk in where we were or what was happening. I understood in my head that this was going to be 'home' for the next few years and that Crazy would probably be with me for a few months (his sentence was bound to be much lighter). But neither of us really knew the full impact of what it all meant. We just put on brave faces and sat quietly – unusual for us because we both normally had something to say or laugh about. But this time there was nothing funny about our situation.

I think it was about 4.30 p.m. when we were let out again for association. As all the cell doors were unlocked, every-body came over to talk to us to find out what we were in for. Most had been acquaintances on the 'out'. It felt quite strange being greeted with a smile and handshake, as if we were being applauded for our misdeeds. They had heard on the radio and seen on local TV that we had been arrested for importation of class A drugs. But quantities had not been mentioned in the reports, so I told them what they were. Straight away they started guessing the length of my sentence, their estimates ranging from three and a half to six years. They added that with good behaviour I might be released after serving one-third of my time. In my heart I had already prepared myself for six years. Anything less I considered a bonus.

The evening meal was much better than I expected. In fact, prisoners from the mainland would comment that the food in Guernsey prison was haute cuisine compared with what they had been used to in other prisons. Crazy and I tucked in.

Afterwards, I knew I had to contact my family. I plucked up the courage to phone my dad.

'Hi, Dad, you know what has happened to me, then?'

There was an awkward silence, and for the first time in his life my dad was lost for words.

'I'm sorry, Dad.'

After a moment, Dad found some words.

'Rod, can you see now why I tried to warn you away from your friends and the life you have been living? It wasn't that I was interfering, it was because I knew one day we would be having this conversation.'

'I know, Dad.'

'I always said that if this happened, I would not be able to visit you. I hope you understand. The last time I saw my own dad was in a prison. It's just too painful – it stirs up too many memories.'

He told me he would write a letter soon and he asked me to let him know once I had decided on a lawyer.

Next, it was my mum's turn. But as I prepared to dial her number, I remembered what day it was.

It was her birthday.

How could I say 'Happy birthday' on the day she had just

heard that her son was in prison? How could a day like this ever be happy for her?

But likewise, how would she stop worrying herself sick unless she heard from my own mouth that I was OK?

It took me a while to pluck up the courage to dial her number, but eventually I managed it.

'Hello,' she said, in that familiar Welsh accent. It was reassuring to hear her voice.

'Mum, it's me. I'm OK. I'm in prison. And this is the best place for me right now.'

'Rod, what has happened has happened,' she replied, 'and you can't change that. But you can change what happens from now on. I love you, you know that, and as a family we are here for you. Rod, I want you to know that I forgive you and that I'm praying for you.'

I knew she meant it, and those words touched me deeply.

As she had done many times before, Mum began to tell me that God loved me and that he would help me if only I opened up my life to him.

'I'm going to send you some books, Rod – testimonies of gang members and drug addicts whose lives God has completely turned around.'

'I'll read them, Mum, I promise.' Agreeing to read the books was the kindest thing to do under the circumstances and I was prepared to go to any lengths to make her feel better.

'Mum, I'll write to you, and I'll ring you again as soon as I get some phone cards. I'm fine. Please promise you won't worry about me.'

I said goodbye and grabbed a mug of tea before turning in. It was 'bang up' (being locked up for the night) time so I climbed into the top bunk. Crazy had just had a blazing row with his girlfriend on the phone and was trying to get rid of his anger by doing press-ups. I just left him to it and fell asleep.

After a restless night I woke at 7.30 a.m. The cell door opened and it was time for breakfast. I heard that a single cell had become available so I asked one of the officers if I could have it. He said that was fine but I needed to fill in an application form, which I completed immediately. I felt I needed my own space. I wasn't in any state of mind to counsel Crazy on his relationship issues.

Quite quickly I was given the green light and I moved my belongings upstairs, into cell F1. Next door to me was Ian – a man in his forties whose head was covered in tattoos. On first appearance he looked intimidating. In reality, however, he was a top guy and we became good mates, regularly chatting over a coffee and a roll-up. Sadly, Ian is no longer with us. I'll never forget his kindness in those early days in prison.

That evening I had my first visitors in the visitors' room – my brother-in-law, Carl, and my best friend, Hannah. Carl always used to say in jest that I was the brother he never wanted, but he was always there for me when I needed him. He had brought me some clothes, toiletries and books that my mum had given him. He told me that my sister was still coming to terms with what had happened and that in time she would come and see me. There was no problem with me phoning her though.

I could see that Hannah was sad, but she tried her best to be positive and encouraging. She said that her boyfriend and all the 'girls' were asking after me and would write to me soon.

After visiting was over, they both got up to leave. Hannah gave me one of her comforting smiles. 'I'll come and visit again soon. Take good care, Rod.'

I carried the bag of goodies back to my cell. When I looked inside the bag, I discovered that my mum had bought me enough toiletries for about a year (or that's what it seemed like). *Thanks, Mum,* I thought to myself, *you of little faith!*

Also inside the bag I found the books she had promised me. There were three of them: *The Cross and the Switchblade, Run, Baby, Run* and *Chasing the Dragon.*

When I was younger I had heard about the story of Nicky Cruz, one of the most feared gang members in New York City and the subject of *The Cross and the Switchblade* and the author of *Run, Baby, Run.* They had sold over twelve million copies worldwide.

Why are these books so popular?

I was intrigued and now couldn't wait to read them. I had nothing else to do and there were no distractions. I was by myself, so there was no reason not to start reading one of the books.

Two hours later, I was still reading. I was engrossed.

I was totally hooked by the story of Nicky's upbringing in Puerto Rico at the hands of parents who were heavily involved in the occult. I could hardly believe the shocking events he'd witnessed as a child.

I read on to learn about his move to New York in the 1950s and his joining the notorious gang known as the Mau Maus – a gang in which he soon became one of the leaders.

I felt as if I was there as I read about the extreme violence between rival gangs and Nicky's lust for blood and for seeing people get seriously hurt. Anyone who stood in his way would suffer from whatever weapon he had to hand.

Surely this can't be a Christian book.

The following lunchtime I read on. In fact, I couldn't put it down.

Then the story reached the point where I thought it was going to lose my attention – when a preacher showed up and started talking to the gang members about how their lives could be changed. The preacher approached Nicky and told him that Jesus loved him. Nicky threatened to kill him.

Was this preacher mental or what?

There was no way that Nicky was going to listen to him, and there was also no chance, to my mind, that Jesus, if he existed, would want anything to do with a guy like Nicky – not after everything I'd just read.

But the preacher wouldn't let up. He persisted in telling the gang members at every opportunity that Jesus loved them. He just wouldn't quit.

I continued to read that night before falling sleep. I had reached the point in the story where the preacher had arranged a meeting in a church with an open invitation to all gang members. *That was asking for trouble.*

I couldn't wait to continue reading the next morning, so I made sure I got up early.

Some of the rival gang members joined the congregation, including Nicky, who had decided to 'do over' the preacher.

They allowed the preacher to share his message first. He talked about how much God loved them and wanted to change their futures. He told them that God wasn't interested in their past but in their future, that no matter what they had ever done wrong, Jesus had died in their place so that they could be forgiven right there and then.

Reading those words, I began to think about all the bad things I'd done in my life – the drugs, the crime, all the lying and betrayals, and the hurt and devastation I had caused my family.

Could God forgive me for all of this? This deal sounds too good to be true.

I read on.

The preacher finished his message and gave his listeners an opportunity to respond by accepting Jesus Christ into their lives.

Tears began to pour down my face as I read how Nicky Cruz gave his life to God that night. He had entered the meeting intending to kill the preacher. He left with his heart transformed and with a new purpose – to impact others with the love of Jesus as radically as he had just been impacted. Other gang members responded in the same way.

As I lay there in the darkness of my cell, I began to think about Nicky's transformation, and I was jealous of the freedom he had received.

Is this freedom really available to everyone?

I could tell something was going on in my heart. It felt softer.

Is this God?

As the weeks passed by, I continued to read similar books that my dad sent me. In one of his letters he told me that there were people all over the world praying for me. That made me feel important, valued and loved. It really humbled me to think that so many people were praying for Hot Rod, even though they'd never met me. Dad even told me that one of his friends, Gary Raymond from Australia, had had a vision of me leading a Bible study in prison.

What's all that about? I thought.

Receiving and writing letters was something I looked forward to every day. I was fortunate to have a supportive family and some good friends who wrote to me regularly. I was pleased when I received a letter from Joanne, telling me that she was OK and her trip to Thailand had gone well. She told me not to worry if I felt I had let her down. She was very gracious.

The date for my sentencing at the local Royal Court (the equivalent of the Crown Court) was fast approaching. My lawyer had prepared me for a sentence of five years, which was better than my estimate of six.

I phoned Hannah to give her an update.

'Have you heard the news?' she asked.

'What news?' I asked.

'Leon's been found dead in a house in London.'

I didn't know how to respond or what to say. Part of me was really sad; Leon and I had been close mates for many years. My heart went out to his family. But another part of me felt relieved; at least there would be no more threats.

Later, I learned that there were dodgy circumstances surrounding Leon's death. Nothing was ever proved but I had my suspicions. The thought hit me hard that it could easily have been me. If I hadn't been arrested, it might have been my body that had been discovered in that house. The life that had promised everything – money, power, popularity – turned out to deliver nothing.

A few days later, I was still reflecting on this when I heard there was a new remand prisoner called Mickey and that he wanted to see me. I had just finished my work duties for the morning – which consisted of mopping the top corridor and cleaning the officers' toilets – and had returned to my cell.

'Hot Rod, Hot Rod, what are you up to?'

I couldn't help but notice the Brummie accent.

I opened the flap on the door of his cell and there was my mate Mickey, grinning like a Cheshire cat.

'What are you in for, mate?' I asked.

'Fifty-five grams of brown and fifty-six grams of white,'[3] he replied, adding, 'I was stitched up. I'll be getting out of here soon.'

That, however, never happened.

Mickey stayed with us and became the life and soul of the wing. He was someone who truly knew how to brighten up your day. The prison officers didn't feel quite the same way about him and he often found himself in confrontational situations with them. But we loved him. He was generous with all his 'tings', as he called them. He was always good for his 'bacci' and 'bars' (chocolate), especially on a Thursday night when most had run out of theirs and were waiting for the canteen to open on Friday. He would do 'double bubble' deals in which other inmates would have to pay back twice the amount borrowed. I was the only exception to this rule. He was a good mate.

Mickey moved into the cell next to mine when it was made available. By this time I had acquired a mobile phone. When Mickey needed to use it, I would swing it to him out of the

---

[3]   Crack cocaine.

window of my cell using a laundry bag. Mickey would phone his children. He missed them dearly and would call them at least once every day.

'Do you remember that conversation we had down at the Harbour Lights, Mickey?' I asked one evening.

'Yeah, Hot Rod,' he replied. 'I remember it well.'

'If only we had listened to each other and quit what we were doing there and then,' I said.

'Yeah, we should have done it, bruv,' he replied. 'Look at us now, both banged up in prison. If I'm found guilty, I'm looking at twelve years.'

'I know,' I replied. 'I'm looking at five to six. We should have stopped while we could.'

As regrets began to take a deeper hold of me, I couldn't get out of my head the stories I was reading night and day about people whose desperate lives had been transformed and whose past sins had been forgiven. I couldn't stop thinking about Jesus dying on the cross for all my wrongdoings. I had heard the message of the cross many times before in church but had rejected God at the age of 17.

Maybe if I had accepted him then instead of rejecting him, I wouldn't have gone down the road of addiction and crime and ended up in prison.

If God was trying to catch my attention, it was working.

One evening in June 2002, after I had been locked up for the night, I decided to see if this God was real and find out if he'd really accept me with all my mess.

I picked up one of the books I'd read and opened it at one of the pages where there was a prayer which the reader could use to invite Jesus into their life and ask for his forgiveness.

I wanted to do this properly, so I got down on my knees.

I began to read out the prayer, but I soon carried on in my own words.

God, please reveal yourself to me, just as you have to the people I have read about in these books.

Please forgive me for everything I've done wrong in my life, especially for the hurt and pain I've caused people who have loved me.

Forgive me for the destruction I've caused in other people's lives. I'm sorry, God. Sorry for hurting you, too.

Help me to change. Help me to be a better person. Give me the strength to live a different life.

I must have been on the floor for half an hour, crying out to God, hoping he would hear me.

As I finished my prayers and got to my feet, I became aware of what I can only describe as overwhelming love in my heart. I had tried to fill the hole in my soul with wrong things that never brought lasting happiness or fulfilment. There had always been something missing – a deep void in my life. But when I had finished crying out to God, I became instantly aware that something had changed. I understand now that it was God's love that had met that profound hunger. I knew that he had heard my prayer. I knew he had accepted me. I was at peace with God and with myself, and I felt like shouting out, 'Thank you, Jesus! Thank you, Jesus!'

But I kept the cry to myself, expressing it quietly in my heart, as I didn't want my mates to think I had completely lost the plot.

That night, I slept deeply and woke in the morning with what the Bible calls 'a peace that passes all understanding' and what Jesus called 'a peace that the world cannot give'. I felt completely different – content and even hopeful. Something life-changing had happened. I knew without any doubt that this was 'the real deal'.

There was a Gideon Bible in my cell. All the prisoners had one. When I'd tried to read my Bible before, I had found it difficult to understand, but now it was different. I started to read the Gospels and they made sense. They came alive. I couldn't put the Bible down. Sometimes it was as if certain passages jumped out at me, as if God was speaking directly to me through them. And he was.

Day by day, I began to underline verses that spoke to me personally. I had seen my parents do this and had always thought it strange. But now I understood why they did it.

One particular verse that struck me was 1 Peter 1:8: 'Though you have not seen him, you love him; and even though you do not see him now, you believe in him and are filled with an inexpressible and glorious joy.' This was so true. I had not physically seen God, but I knew how real and alive he was, and what I was feeling in my heart was 'inexpressible joy'.

I felt free inside. My external circumstances were far from free. But inside my heart, I knew that I was beginning to experience what Jesus was talking about when he said, 'If the Son sets you free, you will be free indeed' (John 8:36). I had experienced God's forgiveness for my past, and no one could ever have persuaded me otherwise.

I now knew that God had a plan for my future. I didn't know how or when, but I just knew that one day I would help to rehabilitate other addicts. I had a new-found compassion for people and wanted them to experience what I had experienced. I had a genuine sense of hope for the first time in my life, and I didn't want to lose that. It felt so good.

I also began to feel more and more guilty for some of the things I was doing which were breaking the prison rules, including possessing a mobile phone. I gave mine to Mickey. Unfortunately, he was caught with it a few days later and a month was added to his sentence. Really, I should have destroyed the phone and nobody would have got into trouble.

I wrote letters to my family, telling them about my personal encounter with God and my decision to become a Christian. They were really happy to hear the news, although I think my dad was a little sceptical at first. After all, I had conned him on other occasions. It would take time for him to see that my conversion was real.

I kept the news of what had happened to me from my mates for a long while because I didn't want them to think I had gone completely mad. I did try to persuade some of them to read the books I had been given. Some did, but they stopped at 'the God bit'.

I saw God answering my prayers, too. That always amazed me – and still does. I found it simply mind-blowing that the Creator of the universe was listening to me and that I was in a personal relationship with him.

One such prayer was in relation to a large cyst I had on my left cheek. I was due to have an operation to remove it and was told it would leave a scar of approximately two centimetres. Obviously, I wasn't happy about this. One night I asked God to heal me by removing it completely. The next morning when I woke up, the cyst had not gone but had shrunk to a quarter of the size. I kept on looking in the mirror and feeling it – it was definitely smaller. I was excited, but couldn't quite understand why God had not completely healed me. Even the doctor admitted that it had shrunk considerably. I eventually had the operation, which left minimal scarring.

The morning of my sentencing finally came and, surprisingly, I felt totally at peace. While praying about it I sensed God saying 'four years'. With my guilty plea taken into account, as well as the fact that this was my first custodial sentence, I was given four years for the cocaine and six months for the heroin, to run concurrently. So that made four years in total.

Dad, Carl and Emma sat in the gallery as my sentence was passed, hoping that this was the last time they would ever see me in a court room.

Surely this would be the end of all the chaos. With God in my life now, surely I was invincible.

11.

To The Lighthouse

The world is full of fairy tales. One of the most popular finishes something like this: 'and then I became a Christian, and all my problems disappeared.'

Sadly, even though this ending is widely used, it is also an illusion.

We have to be realistic: while becoming a Christian can bring about a radical transformation, it does not mean that our lives become trouble-free. God, by his grace, still allows us to have free will, enabling us to make our own choices, and being human we can, at times, make unwise choices.

Without any doubt I had definitely had an encounter with God. I knew he loved me. I knew he had a plan for my life. I knew how real that change felt in my heart, but God didn't take control over my choices. If I told you that all the decisions I made after my conversion were all good ones and that my life was now perfect, I'd be lying.

I was now in prison serving a four-year sentence. I knew that if I kept my nose clean I'd be eligible for parole one-third of the way through my prison term, which would be July 2003 (this was the case under Guernsey law at the time). This was my goal and I was determined to achieve it.

This meant working closely with the local drug-dependence charity Drug Concern, which provided education and counselling for prisoners who had addictive behaviours. I even enrolled on a counselling course which the educational department of the prison financed. I hoped to equip myself with the skills needed to help others in the future.

My new-found faith was unquestionably helping me through what was a very difficult period of my life. I still had my struggles; I felt vulnerable at times and fell flat on my face more than once. But I took comfort in the fact that God does not promise that we will never face temptation or any trials, but he does promise that he is with us through such times and that his power is available to overcome difficult situations.

Being a new Christian, I was eager to learn more about how to live this out. At the time, there was very little spiritual support, as the Guernsey Prison Fellowship wasn't as established as it is today. There was no Alpha Course or any other course for new Christians to attend. We did have regular Sunday services, where different churches came in on a rota basis. I attended these on occasions. I especially appreciated the support shown to me by a group of elderly ladies who came from St John's Church once a month. They truly exhibited the love of Jesus to me. I wasn't aware of any other inmates who were Christians so I kept my new-found faith a secret for some time. I suppose you could say I was a '007 Christian' – in God's Secret Service – so 'secret', in fact, that no one knew.

I talked with my parents and we concluded that it would still benefit me to go to a Christian rehabilitation centre if my parole was successful. This was discussed with my probation officer, Kerry. Kerry was fairly new to the role but I could see that she had an amazing heart and wanted to help me as much as possible. In fact, I quickly came to see she had compassion and time for all the prisoners.

With the agreement of the prison governor, given that Mum was in very poor health, Kerry made it possible for me to visit her once a month at home for an hour. She also put me forward to go on the work-release scheme which the prison had recently introduced.

Around six months prior to my parole date I was granted work release and was allowed to start at my stepdad's garage, valeting cars, six days a week. This was an immense privilege – very few prisoners got to do this. It also meant I could earn money which I could save up for my release in the future.

A lasting memory of my time working at the garage was when I set myself alight through standing too close to a heater. I didn't notice the inferno behind me and the flames eating through my boiler suit until the mechanics alerted me with a mixture of hysterics and sheer panic. This soon turned into tears of laughter. Well, I was known as Hot Rod, after all.

I couldn't help being excited about the possibility of being accepted for parole. As reports were finalized from all the various agencies I'd been working with – and, of course, from Kerry – I felt I had done more than enough to qualify for early release.

I can't remember the date but I can certainly remember the moment I was called to the deputy governor's office to be told that my parole had been granted and that I would be allowed to leave in a few weeks' time.

I was buzzing. I couldn't wait. Sixteen months in prison was enough for me.

However, although I was elated, I did feel bad for Mickey, who had been sentenced to eleven years. He had pleaded 'not guilty' so received a harsher sentence. He was pleased for me, but it was painful to see that he had so many years left to serve. I vowed to keep in touch with him.

My family and Hannah were the first to hear the good news, as well as some other friends who had been a great support to me, constantly visiting and writing me letters.

It was Friday, 11 July 2003 when I finally walked out of the gates of Les Nicolles Prison a free man.

I must admit, I did smuggle out my Gideon Bible, which I still have today. This was the first Bible through which God really spoke to me, and I didn't want to leave it behind.

For the first time since I could remember I had a meal with my entire family, and it felt so good. It was special. There was no mention of the past. My family had forgiven me for all the things I had done to them. That was amazing.

From that day on, I was able to work at my stepdad's garage until plans were finalized for me to move off the island to begin a rehab programme.

Deep inside me, though, there was a tug-of-war going on.

Part of me knew this was the right thing to do, but another part of me didn't want to leave my family again. Plus, I wanted to enjoy my freedom a bit longer. Going on the programme would mean I'd have to live a disciplined regime for at least another year.

Consequently, I began to convince myself I could engineer my own rehabilitation. I would attend church once a week and keep reading my Bible. Surely this would be enough?

But it wasn't.

As the weeks went by, it wasn't long before I reconnected with some of my old mates who were still into the clubbing and partying scene. Even though I knew it was an unwise move, I decided to meet up with them for one drink.

But this turned into two, then three, and it wasn't long before I got a taste for the old life again.

As I was on parole, I had conditions. In other words, I had to behave myself and not get into any trouble or take drugs – for which I was tested regularly. If I failed, I would be sent back to prison to finish my term.

For a while I passed every test and ticked all the boxes, so Kerry and Gill (my drugs worker) thought that all was going well. They really believed in me. They never thought I would ever foul up again. Nor did my family.

But I did . . . big time.

It was a Sunday in August that same year and I had decided to attend a local event called Vale Earth Fair, which was held at a rundown castle and where bands were playing and what seemed to be unlimited amounts of local ale were on sale. I had managed to get hold of a few Valium, and after a couple of pints I decided to take them. This was a disastrous decision. I soon parted company with my friends and ended up by myself. I decided to leave the event early, get some food and go home in my car.

I drove into the town centre to a fast-food place and ordered chips, cheese and gravy – a personal favourite. I took the food and got back into my car, eating half of it on the way. As I drove off up the hill heading home, I heard a police siren behind me.

I stopped the car and the police bike drew up.

The policeman took off his helmet. I recognized him. It was PC Smith, who had arrested me on a previous occasion.

'Step out of the vehicle, please, sir,' he said.

I complied.

'Have you been consuming any alcohol?'

'I've had a couple of drinks.'

'You've been driving on the wrong side of the road,' he said.

My heart sank.

'I'm arresting you on suspicion of driving while under the influence,' he added.

At that moment, instead of accepting my fate, I made another stupid decision.

I jumped back into my car and drove off as fast as possible. For the next fifteen minutes I was at the front of a high-speed police chase around the island. Recklessly, I raced through red traffic lights, drove on pavements and scraped multiple walls.

I eventually had no choice but to stop when I approached a police road block, screeching to a halt just centimetres away from one of the vans.

Needless to say, I was arrested and later charged for driving under the influence and escaping police custody.

Waking up in the police cell the next morning, I had little recollection of what had gone on, but as soon as I was interviewed it all came flooding back.

History had repeated itself. I could not believe it.

I was released and told that the parole board would be informed. I knew that it was only a matter of days before I was arrested and my parole licence revoked.

I couldn't apologize enough to my family. Once again, they were devastated when they heard what I'd done.

The following day, I met up with my probation officer, Kerry, and she read the police report to me. I could tell she was shocked and saddened by my behaviour.

I was gutted.

Once again, I had let everybody down, especially God. He had given me the opportunity to live a different life. If only I had listened and made good choices. Now I had blown it. Why would God ever want anything to do with me again?

The answer to that question came from an unexpected quarter. One of my mum's cousins, Brian, a pastor of a church in Swansea, was over visiting the family at the time. He reassured me that God had not given up on me and that he still loved me and had a plan for my life. He encouraged me not to stop believing that for myself. This was a real comfort. Brian was visiting at just the right time and became a source of strength and hope for both me and my family.

The day came when I found myself in a police car on the way back to Les Nicolles Prison, less than two months after leaving it. I was greeted by the reception officers. After a very quick induction they took me straight to my cell, which was exactly the same one I was in the first time around. It was strange. What was stranger still was feeling that deep sense of peace once again. I just knew that God was still with me, in spite of the fact that I'd messed up.

By this time, Mickey had been moved to a prison on the mainland to serve the rest of his sentence. Some of my other friends had been released, but there wasn't any shortage of familiar faces, especially one I knew very well – my sister, Emma.

As soon as I had received my original release date, Emma had successfully applied for a job as a prison officer. The only condition was that I would have to be released before she began. When I ended up back in the same prison, it put Emma in a very difficult situation, jeopardizing her new-found career. Emma was away on her training when she heard the news. I can only imagine how she must have felt; her brother was back in prison, and the job she had set her heart on was now looking unlikely.

Fortunately, it was agreed that Emma could continue with the training and that she would still be allowed to work in Les Nicolles Prison. I had mixed emotions. Of course I wanted her to pursue her career, but I was also worried about her seeing me in this environment on an almost daily basis, and I was mortified about the possibility of her having to lock me up at night. I couldn't quite get my head round it. And what were my friends going to say?

My sister recalls her first shift being on my birthday that October. I remember dreading getting out of my cell that morning and walking down the corridor to the hatch to pick up my breakfast in fear of seeing her. But there she was, standing there, smartly dressed in her new uniform, alongside two other officers. She gave me a smile as I walked past, as she did to the other prisoners. I responded with a sheepish grin, feeling very embarrassed and ashamed. It didn't take the other prisoners long to start ripping into me – all in good humour, I might add. As my sister and I are very similar in looks they nicknamed her 'Mrs Hot Rod' instead of Officer Le Page. As Emma has a good sense of humour she wasn't offended. In fact, all my mates and the other prisoners really liked her.

Even though Emma took her role very seriously, she was very kind and caring towards them and enjoyed some healthy banter with a lot of them – especially the Liverpudlians.

Here's Emma's account.

I was nearing the end of my training when I received a phone call informing me that my brother had broken his parole and would be back inside Les Nicolles Prison when I returned from the UK to begin my work as a qualified prison officer in the same prison.

The news was devastating, almost unbelievable. As Rod's sister, I felt overwhelmed with anger and disappointment. I was angry that he'd let the family and himself down, yet again; disappointed, as we'd given him so much support over the years, and here he was, throwing it all back in our faces. It was as if he had no regard or respect for himself or for others.

One of the first times I saw Rod while on duty was during an early-morning shift.

It was breakfast time, and Rod's wing had been unlocked and its inhabitants were ambling along the bottom corridor towards the serving hatch at the other end, eager to collect their bowls of cereal and plates of toast.

This particular morning was 21 October, Rod's birthday. Rod was wearing prison-issue kit, which consisted of a pale blue T-shirt, grey joggers and a burgundy sweatshirt.

Not surprisingly, Rod looked like the majority of the prisoners at Les Nicolles, whose faces wore an empty look and a grey pallor. The monotonous daily routines had become ingrained and this showed in their trance-like demeanour. For one split second, however, I was Rod's sister, Em. As he passed by, a pang of sadness washed over me, but I covered it up with a smile. The awfulness of the situation felt raw and the sight of Rod in shapeless, baggy prison-issue kit was almost heart-breaking.

However, that was the only time I recall that I allowed myself to become Rod's sister instead of Officer Le Page while on duty. When I put on my uniform I became an officer, employed in a professional capacity to provide a duty of care to all prisoners resident at Les Nicolles, and Rod was just one of those prisoners.

Friends have often asked me how it felt having to lock up my own brother. To me, this was a very small part of the job, one of the many routines that I carried out during a shift. That was what it was: just part of my job.

A pragmatic Officer Le Page would think, 'Well, if Rod wasn't in here, he'd probably be dead.' To be honest, it was a relief to know that he was 'inside'.

As for me, I had no choice but to get used to Emma being around and to responding to her as a person with authority over me. She was the one with the keys, and when she was on night duty she would often have to lock the door of my cell.

'Goodnight, Rod,' she would say.

'Goodnight, Em,' I'd reply, before evening 'bang up'.

Even more bizarre was the day I was up in court for having escaped police custody. My sister was on court duty that day and was the one who had to stand next to me in the dock. I was given a three-month custodial sentence to run concurrently and banned from driving for five months. The judge said that this was one of the worst cases of dangerous driving he had ever heard of, calling it 'horrendous driving'. This was not a claim to fame.

As I write this, ten years have passed since that time and it's hard to comprehend that any of it really happened. When I read old press articles and listen to stories from my family and old mates about certain events, I feel a shiver go down my spine. *Surely I wasn't really that bad?*

I think this is because today I am a completely different person from the one I was back then – so far removed from Hot Rod the addict, the dealer, the gambler, the criminal.

You are probably thinking, 'How are you a different person? You messed up again. You were back in prison. You caused hurt and pain to your loved ones again.'

All that is true. I had gone off the rails again, so you could be forgiven for thinking I was the same old Hot Rod. The reality was that, even though by God's grace he had begun a change in me, I had not fully comprehended how powerful the pull back towards my old life would be.

John 10:10 says that the devil's mission is to steal, kill and destroy, but Jesus' mission is to bring life, and life in its fullness. So if Jesus is here to bring new life, this verse clearly demonstrates that the devil's schemes are to oppose this. I was beginning to understand that now. I had come to realize that the devil would throw any obstacle in the way to stop me from finding and fulfilling God's plan for my life. Sadly, so many people are blind to his schemes. But I was becoming acutely aware of them.

I made a decision to follow through on the promptings that I felt God put in my heart, and to do so in complete obedience.

With my parole licence revoked and sixteen months of my sentence left to serve, I became more determined than ever to get a placement on a Christian drug rehabilitation programme. Dad sent me the details of around ten Christian rehab organizations in England, Wales and Scotland. Unknown to me, he had also made enquiries and, in his mind, had decided on one which he strongly felt would be right for me. He didn't share this with me at the time as he did not want to influence my decision in any way.

So I phoned the centres one by one, usually talking to one of the managers, who would go into detail about their programme and what they would expect from me.

They were all fairly similar, to be honest, and as I was coming to the end of the list I was feeling discouraged, as none of them had jumped out at me.

I left it a few days before phoning The Lighthouse Foundation based in Widnes, Cheshire. This was the last one I was going to try.

I got through to the then director, David Tierney, and told him my story. He then told me some of his, as he had once been involved in the criminal underworld in Liverpool. Since his own encounter with God he had helped set up The Lighthouse Foundation in the late 1990s.

David told me about the 'Apprenticeship for Life' programme they ran and it really appealed to me. He said it would be tailored to my needs. He was very encouraging and told me to continue to call back as often as I could.

As soon as I put the phone down I felt God saying to me that this was where he wanted me to go. It's hard to explain, but I just knew that this was the voice of God. My heart was filled with joy and excitement.

I told my dad. It was exactly the same one he had picked.

I continued to phone The Lighthouse, mainly speaking to the manager, Ian Aitken, who was also very encouraging. Ian sent me an application form, which I filled in and returned as quickly as possible.

Ian asked if there was any possibility I could visit The Lighthouse for a face-to-face interview and to see the place for myself. This was normal procedure. As I was in prison in Guernsey, however, it was highly unlikely.

Still, I told Kerry about this opportunity and asked if it would be possible for me to go for an interview. She said it had never been done before but she'd put it to the parole board.

After a couple of weeks praying and waiting I met with Kerry again. Her face was beaming. The parole board, along with the prison governor, had agreed to release me for twenty-four hours so that I could attend an interview at The Lighthouse Foundation. This meant flying to Manchester by myself on the condition that my dad would pick me up from the airport and drop me back after the interview. My dad even sent a letter to the prison governor stating that if I didn't return, he would come over and finish my sentence for me.

Think about this for a moment. Not only was I down as an escapologist in my police file, but just a few months before I had been arrested and charged with escaping police custody. The odds were completely stacked against me. But God had a plan, and he made the impossible possible. I had prayed and prayed, and God had come through for me. And so I was released to attend the interview at The Lighthouse Foundation in March 2004.

Dad met me as agreed at Manchester Airport and we made our way to Widnes. The drive took less than an hour. As we entered the grounds of The Foundry campus, where The Lighthouse Foundation was situated, it seemed a far cry from Les Nicolles Prison. It was also a lot bigger than I'd imagined – six acres of land, to be precise.

In addition to the large building, which I later found out was The Foundry Church, there was also sheltered accommodation, called Fairhaven's Court, comprising forty-five retirement bungalows, all red brick and with neatly kept lawns.

We were directed to The Lighthouse by a lady in reception.

The Lighthouse, at the time, was a large detached bungalow which housed up to five students (it now has two properties and has the capacity to house eight).

On arrival, I felt nervous and apprehensive as I rang the doorbell. We were greeted by David.

I didn't know what Dad was thinking, but as soon as I saw David I thought, 'I don't ever want to get on the wrong side of this guy!'

David was well-built and stocky. He appeared to have no neck and his head was as neatly cropped as the lawns – in fact, 'shaved' is a better word than 'cropped'. Here was a no-nonsense guy, but with a kind spirit behind his tough exterior. David's broad Scouse accent only added to his unusual image.

Once inside, we were shown into the lounge, where we met Ian. This was getting more like 'Meet the Management' by the minute. Ian Aitken, or 'The General', as he was known, was even broader than David and much taller, at around six foot three. His Scouse accent was also strong. Wearing suit trousers and a white shirt, and sporting a neatly trimmed beard and moustache, he could easily have passed for a night-club bouncer or a prison guard.

As soon as the handshakes and even hugs were done, we sat down in the lounge to enjoy a 'brew' (a cup of tea). This was where the interview took place. It was very relaxed and I felt completely at ease. It was here that the programme was explained to me: what I could expect from it and, equally, what they would expect of me. They made sure that I knew this wasn't going to be an easy ride and, in some ways, would be more of a challenge than being in prison. I wasn't put off in the slightest.

'You give me twelve months and your life will never be the same again,' David said.

'Whatever it takes,' I replied. 'I really want this.'

As soon as I'd set foot through the front door of that bungalow I'd felt at peace, and so did Dad. This was the confirmation I needed.

Dad and I were given a tour of the rest of the accommo-dation. I can only describe it as first class and a lot more homely than I'd anticipated. It was smartly furnished, and the students obviously took great pride in keeping it clean and tidy. We also had a walk around the rest of the site.

As we were given the guided tour by David and Ian, it was clear that these two guys had a genuine desire to help others and clearly wanted the best for me, even though we'd only just met. As they were Liverpool FC supporters, I think I secured my place that day after pledging my allegiance to The Kop!

The church building was impressive. I was told that between three and four hundred people gathered in the main auditorium to worship every Sunday morning. It also had a five-a-side sports hall. I even met some of the tenants of the retirement bungalows, including a lady called May Jolly, who was in her late seventies. She embraced me as if she'd known me all her life. Little did she know that one day I would be her chaplain.

Before I left to go back to the airport, David and Ian both prayed for me. I had never experienced anything like that before. I can only describe it as feeling as if the door to my old life was slammed shut in my heart, leaving me ready for whatever new things God had planned for me.

In truth, I knew this was my destiny.

I returned to the prison, and within days I had received a letter from The Lighthouse, offering me a placement upon my release. This was great news, but I still had another nine months to go.

Kerry suggested that, even though it had never been done before, I should apply to the parole board and request early release with conditions. She had spoken with Ian and felt it was a positive move forward. This would mean getting parole twice in the same sentence. I had never heard of this happening. The application was made along with a lot of prayer.

Within weeks, Kerry was once again the bearer of good news. The parole board had granted me early release so that I could start the Lighthouse programme on 1 June 2004. They even gave me a date which was a couple of days earlier than the actual start date, so that I could spend some time with my family before going.

To say that I was ecstatic is an understatement.

I was released on parole for a second time and moved to a place I had never heard of before. I started the rehabilitation programme that was potentially going to last up to two years.

With a mixture of hope and fear, I left Guernsey to start a new life in Widnes. I was determined not to let history repeat itself ever again.

I was off to The Lighthouse.

12.

Taking Hold of My Future

On 1 June 2004 I finally nailed my colours to the mast.

I had tried to live my life as a Christian on my terms, but had failed miserably. I knew I had to hand over every part of my life to God and, to quote the hymn, to say 'I surrender all'. That was scary. But, looking back, it was the best decision I have ever made.

At the age of 26, and having served just over two years in prison, interrupted only by the six weeks I had been out on parole, I was now about to start another type of regime: this time, a programme of rigorous self-discipline and spiritual input designed to equip me to live a life free from addiction. One of the first addictions I tackled was nicotine. I was able to quit smoking on day one. That was a good start.

When I arrived at The Lighthouse to commence the 'Apprenticeship for Life' programme, I was met by David. After our first meeting at the time of my interview it was crystal clear to me that, even if I wanted to, I wouldn't be able to pull the wool over his eyes. This was true of all the staff. They weren't going to be conned or scammed by anyone.

Over the next twenty-four hours I met the other staff and students, all of whom welcomed me warmly and made me feel instantly accepted.

I was allocated my own bedroom, but that didn't mean I slept well – not to begin with, anyway. For the first two weeks I experienced the most horrendous nightmares every night, all of them vivid snapshots from the past.

A student sleeping in the room next door heard me screaming in my sleep. His name was Matthew and he had just finished the programme at The Lighthouse, as had his brother Peter, who was now employed as a support worker. Matthew went on to become a volunteer mentor and was a great support to me. We became good friends. He told me that, during those early days, he would pray for me when he heard me crying out in my sleep. Thanks to his prayers I got through that first fortnight.

With changed lives in evidence all around me, I embarked on the programme with increased hope. Although the daily routine was structured and disciplined, it was not as taxing as prison life had been. Here there were boundaries, but I still had a certain degree of freedom.

All students were encouraged to be involved in the running of the property and we had a plan of daily duties that made up part of the everyday structure. In addition, we also had work-related activities, such as ground maintenance for the elderly at Fairhaven's Court, window cleaning and decorating. Time was also spent developing domestic and practical skills, such as cooking, budgeting, shopping and cleaning. Some evenings we participated in social and recreational activities, such as fitness programmes at the gym and trips to the cinema.

A typical day consisted of a wake-up call at 7.30 a.m., breakfast at 8.15 a.m., morning devotions and Bible study at 9 a.m., house duties at 10 a.m., general duties or appointments at 11 a.m., followed by lunch at noon.

The afternoons were spent on work duties from 1 p.m. till 4 p.m., followed by free time before the evening meal at 6 p.m.

The evenings were set aside for leisure activities, free time or personal study. We would retire to our rooms at 10.30 p.m.

Within this structure I made good use of my free time, spending much of it in my bedroom reading Christian books. I wanted to learn more about my Christian faith and the kind of life that Jesus wanted me to live. I read the Bible most days, and my knowledge and understanding began to grow. I was hungry for more of God in my life, and my passion was fuelled even further about seeing others experience this same freedom.

Then there was The Foundry Church.

I'll never forget my first Sunday service. To say it was overwhelming would be an understatement.

The people were so kind and encouraging. In fact, I don't think I'd ever been hugged by so many people in my life. At first, I was a little uncomfortable with it. But it felt sincere. I was accepted and loved, welcomed into a family.

To begin with, it was strange being in a congregation of three hundred people. The singing was passionate. People were jumping up and down and shouting praises. This was lively to say the least. Deep inside, I wanted so much to join in. Now that I had a personal relationship with God it wasn't like my previous experiences of church, where I just didn't get it. Now I wanted to thank my heavenly Father for what he was doing in my life. And yet, being in a lively congregation was still alien to me. It was a new barrier to overcome.

It took me weeks before I raised my hands in worship, but when I did it felt natural and liberating. God had rescued me from a pit of despair. Lifting my hands was the very least I could do by way of expressing my thanks to him. If people could lift their hands to support their favourite football team or to idolize their favourite pop group, why couldn't I raise my arms to worship the one who gave his life for me, the real deal, Jesus, my rescuer?

The senior leader of The Foundry Church, Brian Hewitt, and his wife, Anne, were a source of great encouragement to me. On one occasion, Brian asked me up onto the stage during a Sunday morning service and prayed for me right there and then, in front of everyone.

Brian has been my spiritual leader ever since. He has never stopped believing in me and has given me countless opportunities, many of them involving significant levels of responsibility.

Other members of staff also came alongside me to support me. I can't express the debt I owe to them. Some are among my closest friends today.

As I progressed through the Lighthouse programme at some pace, it wasn't long before I was given trusted roles within the centre. This included taking on the overall responsibility for the food budgeting and meal planning. I also made up a cooking rota for the rest of the guys on the programme. I enjoyed doing this. I would construct a menu plan on a weekly basis and go out with one of the support workers to buy the necessary food. I was always on the lookout for bargains. I became quite a chef, a skill which I didn't even know I had!

I also picked up basic gardening and decorating skills. I took pride in mowing and strimming the lawns of all the bungalows on site, knowing that this was a great help to the elderly who lived there. They always took the time to show their thanks and appreciation, giving me and the other students bottles of Coke and ice creams.

Every month, I would meet with a staff member from The Lighthouse to review my support plan. On these occasions we would discuss progress made from previous goals, set new targets, and put in place an action plan to help me achieve them. Reflecting each time on what I had achieved since the previous review gave me a great sense of satisfaction, as I could see how far I had come. This helped keep me focused on moving forward to complete the next stage of the programme.

I got baptized on 7 November that year. This was another significant moment in my journey as a Christian. Both my mum and dad were there, and it was a special occasion for them.

After about six months I began to experience, once again, the longing I had experienced in prison two years previously – to help other recovering addicts. Experiencing first-hand the freedom that Christ brings made me want to bring that same freedom to others who were suffering with the same afflictions that I had once had.

There is a story in the Bible (Mark 2) about a paralysed man. When he was brought to Jesus by his friends he received three gifts.

The first thing he received was forgiveness. Jesus said, 'Son, your sins are forgiven.'

The second thing he received was freedom from his disability. Jesus told him to get up from the mat he was on. And he did!

The third thing he received was fulfilment. Jesus told him to walk and take his mat with him. What a miracle!

This third gift is worth thinking about. Jesus wanted the man to enter a whole new dimension of life. He wanted him to take hold of the thing that used to take hold of him. He wanted him to take up his mat to demonstrate his healing and freedom – so that others could see that he was a changed man.

It is one of the greatest joys in the Christian life to be called to break for others the chains that used to bind you. God makes a message out of our mess. He gives us our freedom and then calls us to go back to those who are still in the same kind of captivity and share the good news that Jesus is the real deal. He is the one who can set them free.

That is fulfilment.

When Jesus heals someone of anorexia, they have a testimony which can then break the bondage of those who are still afflicted by this terrible disorder.

When Jesus delivers someone who has been trafficked as a prostitute, he turns them from being a prostitute to being a princess, so that they can then bring the message of freedom to those trapped in this state of oppression.

And when Jesus sets a drug addict free, he does it because he wants them to bring liberation to those who feel powerless in the grip of their addiction.

Before, the greatest desire in my life had been to gamble and take drugs. Now, it was to bring freedom to those whose lives were being destroyed by addiction.

I made this desire known to David and Ian, who encouraged me to pursue whatever God had planned for me. If that was what he wanted me to do, it would happen. 'Just keep your eyes fixed on Jesus, Rod. Don't stop praying and believing, mate.' They said that to me a lot.

I continued to pray and to trust the people God had put in my life. These were people who believed in me, loved me, cared for me, prayed for me and supported me through some of the difficult decisions I had to make while I was there.

They believed in me when I didn't believe in myself. They saw the potential in me that I couldn't see at all. If only everyone had people like that around them.

At the twelve-month mark, David and Ian called me into their office. They told me that one of the support workers, Alan, would soon be moving on and they strongly suggested that I apply for his job once I had graduated. I was over the moon about this opportunity and felt assured once again that God was directing my steps.

While at The Lighthouse I also rediscovered my passion for doing magic tricks, mainly using cards, and most evenings I would astound the other students with my skills. I felt that this was a talent God had given me to both entertain and connect with people.

During my time as a student at The Lighthouse, the spiritual input I received was invaluable in my maturing as a new Christian. Gwen, a retired missionary in her eighties who lived on site at Fairhaven's Court, would come in twice a week and teach on various passages from both the Old and the New Testaments. She would always leave us with notes from her session so that we could study them. Everybody loved Gwen, and that wasn't just because she brought us biscuits and chocolates. She truly knew Jesus in a personal way. I wanted to know him as she did. Gwen became my spiritual mum.

One particular morning, a special guest came in to take the morning devotion. Her name was Kate and she was doing a gap year at The Foundry Church. Kate had shoulder-length brown hair, was of average height, with blue eyes, and she had a lovely smile – although it was a cheeky smile at times, evidence of her fun personality.

That morning, Kate talked about self-worth and read out a poem which I still have to this day. She talked about the importance of seeing ourselves as God sees us because he created us in his likeness. She spoke about how God always looks on the inside of a person, at their heart, and how that was far more important than anything external.

Self-worth was a massive struggle at that time for me, as it is for many. I had come off drugs. The desire to use and to gamble had completely gone, but I had a very negative self-image and found it so hard even to *like* myself. I still had a lot of emotional baggage from my past. Dealing with this was probably the most difficult thing I ever had to do.

As Kate shared about her own vulnerabilities, I respected her honesty and sincerity.

Kate had started her gap year around the same time I started at The Lighthouse. She was a few years younger than me, but whenever we bumped into each other we would have a laugh and a joke.

I remember one Sunday, after the morning service, I took a pack of cards and showed her a trick over coffee and cake. She was impressed.

I became very fond of her – and it wasn't just because of her piercing blue eyes and beautiful smile. I had met many women at the church, but there was something different about Kate. She had a great sense of humour and was always up for a bit of banter. I could also see she really loved God. This was evident in the way she was so kind and loving towards everyone. Every time we chatted I felt happy – something that was clearly visible in the expression on my face and which didn't go unnoticed by some of her friends!

It's fair to say that I couldn't help feeling affection for her.

When I visited Wales to attend my gran's funeral in Saundersfoot, I bought Kate some fudge and a tea towel that was emblazoned with the Welsh flag. This was partly to be a bit cheeky, but when I gave them to her I noticed that she blushed and she wasn't sure how to respond. I thought either I had blown it or that this was a sign that she felt the same way towards me. I hoped and prayed it was the latter. I was only a couple of months away from completing the programme at The Lighthouse and wanted to remain focused.

I graduated from the 'Apprenticeship for Life' programme at The Lighthouse Foundation in November 2005 and I applied for the role of support worker as encouraged by David and Ian. I was successful and started my new job as a salaried full-time support worker from January 2006. It was sad to see Alan leave, as we had established a good friendship. In fact, two years later he asked me to be his best man at his wedding. I felt so privileged to be asked as I had only known him for a short time.

With the start of my new role as a support worker, God had given me the desires of my heart (Psalm 37:4). This was my opportunity to start making a message out of my mess. This was my chance to take hold of what had taken hold of me, telling others, 'Look what Jesus has done for me!'

I had been set free from my addictions and had seen many broken relationships restored. I now had renewed hope for the future. The programme had allowed me to create a platform upon which I could rebuild my life and start to develop character, to nurture healthy relationships, to mend broken relationships and to gain a vision for my future. I could tell that God was beginning to work out the plan he had to prosper me . . . to give me a hope and a future (Jeremiah 29:11).

Following my graduation in 2005, I moved into shared accommodation with another former student. Kate had also graduated from her gap year and was in the process of deciding what to do next with her life. This meant it was possible that she might leave the area completely. I prayed that Kate would stay around – a selfish prayer, I know.

I eventually plucked up the courage to invite Kate over for a meal and a movie. During the few hours we were together I just knew that she was the girl for me. I did almost blow it when I made her watch a documentary on Guernsey – not the most romantic move in history, nor one which provoked much of an enthusiastic response in Kate! It was therefore a good job she was impressed with my culinary skills. We both wanted to see each other again. We even had a sneaky kiss before she left.

After many texts and conversations over the next few weeks, we decided to make it official. Everybody was really encouraging and supported us in our decision.

As I got to know Kate more and more, my relationship with her family also grew.

I was slightly nervous about the fact that Kate's dad was a crime prevention officer. This could have been awkward. However, Paul (Kate's dad) had been a volunteer at The Lighthouse so had seen me progress throughout my time there. I could see that both Paul and Kate's mum, Di, were very special people. They accepted me immediately and I felt part of their family very quickly. They also attended The Foundry Church.

There was a surreal moment when I learned that Paul's surname was Daniels. Yes, he was called Paul Daniels – the same name as that of the magician I used to watch as a child and who was an inspiration behind my magic tricks. God clearly has a sense of humour!

Kate and I were engaged in March the following year and married in January 2007. What a special day of celebration that was – one I will never forget! By the grace of God I had found my lifelong companion.

I worked for The Lighthouse for just over four years, and in that time I witnessed many people being set free from drug and alcohol addiction. I also had the opportunity to go back into Les Nicolles Prison in Guernsey and share my story and even lead a Bible study. I could not believe how responsive people were, including some of my old friends. My dad reminded me of the vision that his friend in Australia had had when I was first arrested: that one day I would lead a Bible study in prison. This blew me away.

Towards the end of 2008 I was given a book entitled *Nevertheless*, the life story of John Kirkby, who started a debt-counselling charity called Christians Against Poverty (CAP). I had first heard of CAP some months before while visiting a church in the Midlands called Renewal Christian Centre. This large church was led by Bishop David Carr and his then associate, Pastor Richard Taylor (who now heads up the Victory church network, is the executive director of Victory Outreach UK in South Wales, and who had a very similar background to mine). I enjoyed listening to their teaching on CDs and DVDs. Their honesty and no-nonsense style of preaching inspired me even more to pursue the life that God had for me. I heard about the CAP ministry which they ran and how people were being released from the effects of poverty, and I felt compelled to find out more.

Reading *Nevertheless* completely ruined me. I would stay awake at night as the reality hit me that there were people in my own community who were contemplating suicide because of the hold that debt had on them. Parents were missing meals so that their children could be fed. Sometimes their children had to miss meals too. Married couples were separating because of the stress of debt. This was not right. I had to do something. I felt such a burden in my heart for these people.

I approached the leadership team at my church and told them about the work of CAP. As it turned out, they were feeling passionate about the whole area of debt relief too, so were keen to look into it. If they did decide to set up a CAP centre, they would need somebody to manage it. Was my time at The Lighthouse coming to an end? I prayed and prayed to God for direction and for assurance that this was where he was leading me. I felt frustrated inside about not knowing and not having a clear answer back. All I knew was that my heart was moving towards this work.

On another visit to Renewal Christian Centre, this time on a Tuesday evening for their 'Ministry of Power' meeting, I took the students from The Lighthouse Foundation. At the end of the meeting Bishop David Carr called the Lighthouse students to the front of the congregation which numbered about six hundred people. He began to speak to them one by one, telling them what he felt God was saying to him about their lives. He was completely spot on. I couldn't believe it. Then he called me over, and not knowing what was on my heart he said, 'What you are doing now is great, but God is moving you on to something new. God has heard your prayers, so don't worry, and stop getting frustrated. You will have an answer in December' (this was in the September). This was not guesswork: this man of God was truly hearing from the one he was representing. I held on to that word and couldn't wait to tell Kate. She was excited, and it certainly put my mind at rest. God was in control.

That December, it was agreed by the leadership of The Foundry that a CAP centre would be opened, and I was offered the position of centre manager on a part-time basis. After prayerful consideration I accepted this position. It meant that my job at The Lighthouse Foundation was coming to an end.

Besides my new role as CAP centre manager, The Foundry also employed me to work one day a week as the chaplain for Fairhaven's Court, where I would visit the sick and lead weekly Bible studies in one of the tenant's bungalows. About a dozen of us would congregate in the small lounge and we would spend time singing, praying and discussing the Bible. Included in the group was Gwen, my spiritual mum, and others who had known God for many years. These meetings were far from dull – in fact, I don't think I have ever seen such passion for God and his word as was evident in the lives of these elderly people. Who would have thought that an ex-addict would be used to fulfil this kind of role?

In November 2010 Kate was also employed by The Foundry Church as the scheme manager/warden at Fairhaven's Court. This meant we also got to work together as part of the same team.

After my first year of managing the CAP centre in Widnes we won 'Best New Centre of the Year Award'. This was a real achievement and another example of God's goodness at work in my life. Not long after this, I was also offered an area manager position with CAP, covering part of the North-West and North Wales region. I was delighted to accept this offer of increased responsibility and the new challenges that would come with it.

As I write this, I have been working for CAP for five years and we have just held a special service at The Foundry Church celebrating all the lives that have been touched, changed and transformed through this local centre. I have seen not only many families become debt free (by setting up a debt-management plan and providing budgeting advice), but also many people find true freedom through coming to know Jesus Christ as their own personal Saviour. For me, this is what it is all about.

To think that God would use me to bring financial freedom to people's lives after I had squandered more money (through gambling and drugs) than most people earn in a lifetime again just demonstrates that God uses our past failures for future successes.

As I write, it is fast approaching June 2014, which means that it has been ten years since I left Guernsey – ten years in which I have been completely free from my addiction to illegal substances.

As I reflect on everything that has gone on in that decade – the opportunities I have had, the things I have achieved, and the people who have believed in me – I feel completely overwhelmed. Most of all, I am eternally thankful to God that he would choose to use me despite my past failings.

I am reminded of one of the first sermons I heard from Pastor Richard Taylor, entitled 'His Love Qualifies the Disqualified'. This really spoke to me and assured me that no matter what my past had been like, God still wanted to use me, and it was nothing to do with my history but everything to do with his unconditional love. Human beings might focus on my 'disqualifications' – my addictions, crimes, prison sentences and so forth – but God focuses on our future potential, not our past failings.

If you are in a situation similar to the one I was in, in a place of utter turmoil and despair, please don't give up hope. God loves you so much and he does have a plan for your life. If you give him a chance, he can turn your mess into a message, just as he did with me.

Remember, his love is unconditional. It is his love that enables you to be used for his plans and purposes, if only you give him a chance. I challenge you to prove me wrong.

A press reporter once asked me what the secret ingredient was in breaking the cycle of addiction and how I was able to move forward from that place of brokenness to the place of restoration.

My answer was simply 'God', and of course that is so true. Yet at the same time it was up to me to make the right choices together with God's help. I had to choose. You have to choose. We cannot remain in a victim state. We have to rise up, seize hold of our responsibility, and make wise decisions if we are to turn from victims into victors.

I rejected God when I was 17, but when I chose to accept him in June 2002, my life began to take a turn in a different direction. It was the best and most important decision I have ever made.

You too can make this same decision. God doesn't force you to make the choice to follow and trust him. This has to come from you. You have to make a decision, and you have to make it yourself, just as I had to.

This decision has changed not only my life but also the lives of my mates, Lennie and Mickey. You can read Lennie and Mickey's accounts of their personal stories below. I hope you will be encouraged by their stories too to see that Jesus surely is the real deal.

Lennie's Story

I thought it was going to be just another ordinary night out getting off my face on Ecstasy and alcohol, but I ended up in a club bumping into a guy who was known as Hot Rod.

I was on the lookout for Es, and Hot Rod had a reputation for selling pills, so I approached him to buy some.

He told me he could get me a few at £25 each, so I handed him over some money. He went off and returned later with the pills.

It didn't take me too long to work out that he had ripped me off, selling me dud pills. I was not happy. However, little did I know that meeting Hot Rod would eventually end up changing my life for ever.

We met again in the bookies the next day, where Rod paid me back some of the money. He had just won on the horses. I lost the £50 within minutes.

We had a lot in common, including gambling. A friendship was formed from that moment and the bookies became our regular meeting place. We were both heavily involved in the drugs scene, too – basically, anything that involved making money.

Rod had to bail me out on many occasions. When you're involved with drugs and owe money to the wrong people, things can get really nasty and people can get hurt.

Being involved in this lifestyle became unbearable, even to the point where I contemplated suicide. The constant feeling of emptiness and misery was no life whatsoever. I remember Rod supporting me through this difficult period, even though his life was messed up at this point too.

My childhood was not the best, to say the least. I endured serious abuse from a young age. I believe this shaped who I was by the age of 14, which was when I started going off the rails. I was a weak and vulnerable young adult with no future, no prospects and no hope for a better life. I made a decision to do things my way, no matter what harm it was going to cause me or my family.

In my late twenties, after being arrested countless times and even spending time in prison for minor drugs offences, I really did think this was what the rest of my life was going to be like because I couldn't see any way out of the hole I was in.

Then, one day, I heard that Rod had been caught with drugs and had been sentenced to four years in prison. I was gutted, but it meant that I had a chance to focus on making positive changes. To be honest, we had been a bad influence on each other.

I did not hear from Rod for a couple of years as I had moved to England to live with my sister. I was in a bad place again with drinking and gambling. But then, one day, a letter from Rod appeared out of nowhere. He had sent it six months earlier, but it couldn't have arrived at a better time. My life had not changed except to get worse in every possible way. I was probably at the lowest point I had ever been. Rod told me how he had become a Christian and how God had changed his life. He said that God had a plan for my life, too. I thought he was on the wind-up.

Rod also said he was out of prison and in a place called The Lighthouse Foundation in Widnes, which helped and supported men with addictive behaviours. He said that it could help me if I needed it.

I arranged to go and visit Rod, and I was absolutely gobsmacked when I saw him and how he was. This was no wind-up. Rod had changed. It was a miracle.

'It's going to take me six months to get to know you again,' I said.

If this could happen to Rod, it could happen to anyone.

I left wanting what Rod had found, so applied for a placement on their residential programme. Within a couple of months I was accepted by the management of The Lighthouse and moved in.

I will never forget the train journey to The Lighthouse. I was in tears all the way there. My tears were tears of hope. This was the first time I had felt there was any hope for me.

When I arrived at The Lighthouse it took me some time to settle in as I had to fit into a structured regime – something that I had not been used to before. Rod had started working there and was one of my support workers – what a complete turnaround!

I also went to church for the first time. This was an overwhelming experience.

As a result of seeing the change in Rod and the genuine love of the people around me, I began to open my heart to God.

Then, on 3 August 2006, I was asked if I wanted to accept Jesus into my life. I said 'yes' as I had nothing to lose and everything to gain. Rod and other staff members prayed with me that night.

Everybody was so excited about the decision I had made, and from that moment I began to feel different. There was now a purpose for my life. I had been rejected as a child, but now I knew I was accepted by my heavenly Father. I felt his love for me.

Since then, I have had my ups and downs, but as I write this, in December 2013, I have never before felt so free inside or as happy as I am now. Not only have I been able to address my substance-misuse issues, but also, through the amazing work of debt-counselling charity CAP (Christians Against Poverty), I am now completely debt free.

My passion in life now is for others to experience the same.

I can see now that God has used Rod and his remarkable story to impact my life, and I will be eternally grateful for that.

Mickey's Story

I first met Hot Rod through a mutual friend, Jamie, who was a friend of my daughter's mother. The reason for the meeting was to sell him cocaine. We became good friends almost immediately.

I lived in Birmingham but would frequently visit Guernsey to visit my children and to make money by selling drugs.

I wasn't a big user myself. I enjoyed the odd spliff and line of coke, but that was about it. For me, drugs were about the money and because I wanted people to think I was 'the man'. I liked wearing expensive clothes and jewellery and got a buzz from ordering bottles of champagne in night-clubs and giving them out to the ladies.

I had come from a broken home and others in my family were also into the drugs scene. Where I was brought up in Birmingham it seemed to be the normal thing to do.

Even though I had the gold and the expensive clothes, there was something deep down that was missing. I thought that having more money was the solution. I even ended up selling weed for Rod to make more cash.

I'll never forget the conversation Rod and I had at the Harbour Lights pub in March 2002, when we talked about how rubbish our lives were and how we intended to change. However, that did not happen immediately. I soon heard of Rod's arrest for his importation of heroin and crack cocaine. You would have thought that would have stopped me doing what I was planning. It didn't. Not long after this, I ended up being arrested on suspicion of importing £50,000 worth of class A drugs into Guernsey.

This was probably the most chaotic time of my life. I was angry and in denial and pleaded 'not guilty' throughout my trial, even though there was sufficient evidence against me. I ended up getting sentenced to eleven years in prison.

I let a lot of people down, including myself and all my children. It was very difficult to come to terms with.

I ended up being in the cell next door to Rod, and our friendship continued. I remember him telling me he had found God and that he was going to go to The Lighthouse

Foundation on his release. I was pleased for him because I knew deep down he was a good guy.

When he left, we remained in contact, even when I was shipped out to a prison on the mainland. He would write me letters, encouraging me and telling me what God was doing in his life and that he was praying for me. I had been brought up as a Catholic and my gran was a Christian. I never followed in her footsteps, although I did believe there was someone out there.

Rod visited me when I was in Featherstone Prison in Wolverhampton. I had served almost six years by this point. I could see that he had changed and that he wasn't the same crazy old Hot Rod. He even brought me a Bible.

When I was eventually released I made contact with Rod again and went to visit him where he lived. I even went to his church. I enjoyed it.

He later invited me to a conference in Birmingham where an evangelist called Reinhard Bonnke was preaching. I agreed to go. That night, I heard the message of Jesus preached like never before and there was something special in the atmosphere.

At the end of the meeting, Rod asked if I wanted to give my life to Jesus. I said 'yes'.

He prayed with me, and from that very moment I felt a peace in my heart I had never felt before.

I started reading the Bible, even attended church and began to see God answer my prayers.

My friend who was with me that same night also became a Christian, and her life has changed too.

God has used Rod to influence me for good, and my heart's desire is now to do the same for others.

I would like to thank God with all my heart. With him, all things are possible.

Epilogue: Coming Home

If my story has revealed anything, it is the tragic fact that there are many people who are bound by addictions and whose lives are broken, lost and full of despair.

Where can they find help?

The answer which my testimony provides is this: they can be rescued and can find freedom and hope in the love of their heavenly Father.

'OK,' I hear you say, 'don't talk to me about "father" – I never had one/didn't like the one I had. Father? No way!'

Well, read on . . .

Jesus said that he is the way, the truth and the life. No one comes to the Father except through him (John 14:6). The words 'the truth' can also be translated 'reality'. In other words, Jesus is the real deal.

Through the ultimate sacrifice that took place 2,000 years ago – Jesus dying on the cross and letting his own blood spill for the sins of all mankind – it is now possible for us to receive forgiveness, have that sin barrier in our lives removed and have a personal relationship with God. In other words, the cross has bridged the gap between man and God.

Jesus is the only way to the Father. He alone tells the truth about God, that he is our Father. He alone gives us the life that the Father longs for us to live, a life full of purpose and hope.

Nowhere is this made clearer than in the short story Jesus told of the lost son in chapter 15 of Luke's Gospel.

There he describes the younger of two sons who rebelled against his father. He did this by telling his dad that he wanted his inheritance there and then, while his father was still alive. That was a scandalous thing to ask. It was effectively the same as saying, 'I wish you were dead, Dad.'

The father was very patient and kind. He let his son have what he wanted. The son then went off into what Jesus calls 'a distant country' and spent all his money on addictions and wild living. We know that at least one of these addictions was sexual. He spent his father's money on prostitutes.

In the end, his money and luck ran out and he was forced to look for a job. He found employment in a pigpen. For a Jewish boy, that would have been utterly degrading. Pigs are regarded by the Jews as unclean animals.

Then, one day, having hit rock bottom, the lost son came to his senses. He had an awakening. He thought to himself, 'I'll go home to my dad.'

So the son humbly made the long journey back home, not knowing how his father was going to react.

The son needn't have worried, because all along his father had been waiting and watching out for his return. Then, from a distance, he saw his bedraggled son limping home. He ran to his son, threw his arms around him and welcomed him home with tears of joy.

'My son who was lost is found!' he exclaimed. 'I thought he was dead, but he's alive!'

What a picture! What a homecoming! What a dad!

And it's the dad who is the hero of the story, the true focus of the tale.

Notice that he didn't ask where his son had been, he didn't reject him because he had messed up, and he didn't show any anger towards him. What he did do was show compassion and love by restoring his son back into the family home.

This is a true picture of how God, our heavenly Father, sees us. He is the most loving father in the universe, and he embraces those who come back to him, even when they smell of the 'pigpen'.

The reason I am able to write this book and tell you my story is because I have experienced God, my heavenly Father, in just the same way the lost son did in this story. I went searching for fulfilment, satisfaction, contentment and answers, but I was always looking in the wrong places. I thought drugs, money and wrong relationships would fill the emptiness that was in my life. My pursuit of these things brought the complete opposite. Admittedly, for a moment it felt good – but it didn't last, and the end result was pain, hurt, depression, prison and separation from my loved ones. That was not the heart of God for me. That is not the heart of God for you, either.

One thing I know for sure is that when I humbly came to my senses in my prison cell in June 2002 and asked God for forgiveness, I didn't feel condemned in any way. I didn't feel judged – instead I felt complete love and acceptance.

When Jesus died on the cross, he didn't die pointing the finger. He died with his arms spread wide, ready to embrace those who would come to him. He even prayed for those who had put him on the cross, saying, 'Father, forgive them, for they do not know what they are doing.'

What amazing grace!

It is true to say that many fall into an addictive lifestyle because they are hungry for a father's love. We live in a father-less generation, and so many people are searching to fill the void created by the absence of their biological dad (or mum, in some cases).

But the good news is that Jesus is the real deal. He is who he says he is, and God really is the Father that Jesus tells us he is. In other words, God really is an accepting, trustwor-thy, faithful and affectionate dad who will never abandon or abuse us. This may sound too good to be true – but it IS true.

Regardless of whether you're trapped in an addictive lifestyle, in a pit of despair, in a prison cell, or simply feel that there is something missing in your life, I want to encourage you to take a step towards the love and forgiveness that God wants you to receive.

As you take that step of faith, not only will you find salva-tion, but God will begin a process of releasing you from your addictions, healing your emotions, restoring your relation-ships, and giving you a hope and a purpose for your future.

The choice is yours, and I urge you not to hold back any longer. You can have a relationship with your heavenly Father through Jesus Christ by taking the following steps.

First of all, do what the lost son in Luke 15 did. Recog-nize and admit that your life is a mess. Understand that sin – deciding to go your way rather than God's way – has led you into trouble. Admit it. Confess it.

Secondly, say thank you to Jesus for paying the penalty for your sins by dying on the cross. He chose to take the rap for you because he loves you so much. Ask him now to forgive you for all your mistakes. Receive his forgiveness. You don't deserve it, and nor do I. But Jesus wants you to have it.

Thirdly, ask Jesus to come into your heart and fill it with his love. His Holy Spirit longs to dwell in you. Let him in. He is the power of God's love, changing us from spiritual orphans into his adopted sons and daughters. As you welcome the Holy Spirit, the healing will begin so that you can learn to enjoy the glorious freedom of being a child of God.

Don't hesitate. Don't hold back.

Maybe you are right now at the moment of decision.

If you are, pray this prayer:

Dear Father God, I believe Jesus died for my sins so that I could be forgiven and have a relationship with you. Jesus, I want to accept this gift of new life that you want to give me. Please forgive me for all my sins and give me the power to turn away from those things that I know are wrong. Come into my heart as my friend and Lord, and fill me with the Holy Spirit, so that I might know the perfect Father personally. In Jesus' name, Amen.

If you have just prayed that prayer and meant it, tell someone else who is already a committed Christian. Join a church where the people praise God with passion and the Bible is taught without compromise.

Start talking to your heavenly Father in prayer.

Buy your own Bible and begin reading it, starting with the Gospels in the New Testament.

If you do these things, you too will begin to discover that Jesus is the real deal, and that over the course of our lives he really does make a message out of our mess and turns our trials into a testimony.

Remember that making this 'decision' is the first step in the process of living for God. The decision is a one-off; following Jesus and shunning the old life is an everyday experience. The rewards? You'll discover them for yourself, just as I, Lennie, Mickey and countless millions around the world have done.

Finally, if you are a parent whose son or daughter has become trapped in a toxic lifestyle, far away from God, don't lose hope. Take heart from the way God answered my parents' prayers.

In particular, find great encouragement from my mother's testimony of persevering in prayer. Here is her message of hope.

Finding out that your son or daughter is a drug addict and a criminal has to be one of the most heart-wrenching things you can experience.

In this case, it was my son, Rod.

Up until his mid-teens there were no signs whatsoever that Rod would start on the path he chose. We had always had a good relationship and were a close family. I was overprotective of Rod from when he was very young because I loved him and didn't want any harm to come to him.

When I first heard the news about the trouble Rod was getting into and witnessed our house being raided by Guernsey customs officers (on a number of occasions), it hit me that this was serious. I was overwhelmed with worry and concern because I cared for him so much. But I felt helpless because this life Rod was living was alien to me, so I couldn't fully understand why he was doing what he was doing. Every time I tried to talk to Rod he would change the subject and walk off.

'Everything will be all right, Mum, don't worry,' he would say.

I couldn't help imagining Rod one day being found dead somewhere. I barely slept. I suppose this is what all family members go through when their loved ones are involved in such things.

We lost regular contact when he moved out of our house. During this period I became ill, living with the debilitating symptoms of a brain tumour, a subsequent emergency operation to remove it, and the mini strokes that were to follow. During the recovery process, which took many months – even years – my family kept a lot of what was going on in Rod's life away from me, for my own protection.

I had no idea just how deeply involved he was in drugs and crime until one day I heard the news that he had been arrested for importing drugs into the island and was facing a term in prison.

I then received a phone call from Rod telling me what had happened and how sorry he was for letting me and the family down. Even though it was heartbreaking to hear my son's voice from prison, I couldn't help but feel love and compassion for him. Yes, I was disappointed, hurt and still trying to come to terms with what had happened. But this was my son. I also had a sense of hope that everything would be OK. I had been a Christian for over twenty years and my faith had helped me through lots of trials. I knew how powerful prayer was, so I didn't stop praying for Rod.

During one such prayer time, God took me to a verse in Isaiah 44:3, where it says, 'I will pour out my Spirit on your offspring.' I clung on to that promise, and it brought great comfort and helped me through what was a very traumatic time.

I sent Rod books of stories similar to his – stories which had positive outcomes. He promised to read them. Then, a few months later on one of Rod's home visits, he handed me a letter and said, 'You'll be pleased when you read this, Mum.'

In the letter, Rod told me that he had become a Christian and now knew that God was real and that he had a plan for his life. My heart was filled with joy! I couldn't stop thanking God for answering my prayers!

I am still amazed – over ten years on – at what God has done in and through Rod and by the many people's lives that have been impacted as a result of his story.

One thing I have learned through this is to never give up hope.

There is always hope.

Looking for Help

If you are suffering from the effects of substance misuse and have a strong desire to break the cycle of addiction in your life, the following drug rehabilitation centres have a proven success rate and are able to assist in your recovery:

The Lighthouse Foundation (based in Widnes) –
  www.lighthousefoundation.org.uk
Teen Challenge UK – www.teenchallenge.org.uk
Victory Outreach UK (based in South Wales) – www.vouk.
  org.uk
Victory Outreach Manchester – www.vomanchester.com/
  recovery-homes
Betel UK – www.betel.org.uk
Yeldall Manor (based in Reading) – www.yeldall.org.uk

If you would like advice concerning debt and other money-related problems, award-winning national charity CAP – Christians Against Poverty – can help.

Christians Against Poverty works across the UK to release people from a life sentence of debt, poverty and its causes. Working through a network of local churches, they provide free debt counselling, money education courses, job clubs and help with addictions. They offer their services in partnership with local churches because they believe the church holds the only message that can truly transform lives. Each year over 27,000 people find their way out of the black hole of debt through their free debt counselling service, and over 10,000 people are learning to budget, save and prevent debt through the CAP Money Course. They have recently launched CAP Release Groups to help bring freedom to people with addictions. For more information, or to search for help near you, visit capuk.org. For help with unmanageable debts, call their Freephone number on 0800 328 0006.

About the Author

Rod Williams is a passionate evangelist and a graduate of Reinhard Bonnke's School of Evangelism. He and his wife, Kate, work for award-winning charity Christians Against Poverty, based in Bradford.

For further information and details on forthcoming events that Rod will be involved in, please visit www.therealdeal.org.uk.

If you would like to book Rod to speak at an evangelistic event or conference, please email him at info@therealdeal.org.uk.